THE ESTHER FAST MANDATE

THE ESTHER FAST MANDATE

by CLYDE WILLIAMSON *with* JAMES CRAIG

A Call to End-Time Intercession for the
RELEASE
RETURN
RESTORATION &
REVIVAL OF
ISRAEL &
THE CHURCH

ALMOND PUBLICATIONS
Box 336, Etobicoke, Ontario, Canada   M9C 4V3

Copyright 1987 ALMOND PUBLICATIONS

ISBN 0-921715-00-5

Published by ALMOND PUBLICATIONS
Box 336, Etobicoke, Ontario, Canada   M9C 4V3

Cover: Ric Riordon

Printed in Canada
Harmony Printing Limited
123 Eastside Drive, Toronto, Ontario M8Z 5S5

All scripture references unless otherwise stated are taken from *The Holy Bible, New International Version*, © 1978 by the New York International Bible Society.

Dedication

To my beloved Marion,
and our daughters, Karen and Kim,
who have shared not only the vision,
but the calling
that God has placed upon my life to
"Give Him no rest,
till He establishes Jerusalem
and makes her
the praise of the earth." *(Isaiah 62:7)*

To five beloved friends,
Esther, Joe, Jacques, Jim, and Jean
whom the Lord sent at crucial periods
to enable the vision and the call of this mandate
to come forth.

Contents

Foreword

In 1965 I was introduced to a fine couple, Clyde and Marion Williamson, while pastoring Calvary Church in Peterborough, Ontario. They were attending Bible College at that time and made Calvary their home church. Clyde assisted in our ministry for one year and it was at that time we recognized the unusual calling of God upon his life.

Ten years later, in 1975, although we had been out of contact with Clyde for some time, he spent three days in our home in Halifax, Nova Scotia. Clyde felt led of the Lord at that time to go on an absolute fast without food and water according to Esther 4:16. These three days proved to be most significant in the spiritual direction of his life.

In 1982, Clyde became part of the pastoral staff here at Queensway Cathedral in Toronto. It was during this time that his unique call to Israel and the Church became evident to us. Clyde is highly esteemed by his associates and by those whom he has served in ministry.

At the beginning of 1983, the Lord called our church to a forty-day fast. Thirteen days into the fast, on Sunday, January 23, Merv and Merla Watson and Jan Willem van der Hoeven from the International Christian Embassy in Jerusalem were special guests in the evening service. During that service, Clyde Williamson gave a prophetic word in which we were challenged to bless Israel. This would be one of the keys to seeing the outpouring of revival. The call given was to observe an Esther Fast. This call was directed towards our church, our nation, and the body of Christ around the world. *The Esther Fast Mandate* tells the dynamic true story of how believers in seventy-three countries joined in a three-day fast for the Release, Return, Restoration, and Revival of Israel and the Church. This call to prayer arose from a burden in the heart of Clyde Williamson. This book relates how the Holy Spirit is continuing to call the body of Christ to observe the Esther Fast every year until Messiah comes. Your heart will quicken in response to this call as you read this exciting story of God's supernatural direction.

Pastor Ralph Rutledge
Queensway Cathedral,
Toronto
January, 1987

CHAPTER ONE

Pray for the Peace of Jerusalem

It was about 4 a.m., May 8, 1978. I awoke suddenly. My mind was clear and filled with a sense of awe. The Spirit of God had just spoken to me. I was to pray for the peace of Jerusalem.

The thing that got my attention was the reference for those words, "Pray for the peace of Jerusalem" found in the book of Psalms. It flashed through my mind that I had left a Bible on the refrigerator the evening before. Quietly, I rolled out of bed, not wanting to disturb my wife, Marion. I was filled with a sense of anticipation. But I was also puzzled. Why was God asking me to pray for the peace of Jerusalem? I turned on the kitchen light and reached for a Roman Catholic version of the Bible that a friend had loaned me just the day before. Sure enough, the reference of the dream took me right to the passage. It was Psalm 121:6.

As the Minister of Follow-up for Canada's only daily Christian television program, "100 Huntley Street," I could hardly wait to share this special prayer request with the staff in morning devotions. The opportunity came two days later. Upon arrival at "100 Huntley Street," which is the address as well as the name of the program, when I opened my King James Version, I was

9

in for a shock. I looked up Psalm 121:6 only to find it was the wrong verse. I eventually found the reference in Psalm 122:6, but what had happened the night of my dream? The reference I had received was definitely Psalm 121:6 and it had said, "Pray for the peace of Jerusalem." I was delighted to learn the answer some time later. Apparently, some of the Psalms are numbered differently in the Roman Catholic Bible.[1] This knowledge confirmed to me that God had truly spoken and I was not simply remembering a verse I had read previously. That Roman Catholic Bible was only in my home for a few days, and yet, when God chose to call me to pray for Israel, he gave me a reference that would have been meaningless in any other Bible I have ever owned. He knew what Bible I would pick up when I awakened from my dream. I knew that I was being supernaturally directed. It also showed me that God was not prejudiced. From that day on Marion and I began to pray for Israel.

It amazed us to see what God did as we obeyed His request. As the days and months went by, we began to wonder if we were to do more than simply pray. We found we had a deep yearning to go to Israel. As those who believe that prayer should lead to action, we began to ask the Lord if He wanted us to visit the Holy Land.

One day in April, 1979, a very close friend spoke to me and said, "I have one word from the Lord for you, Clyde – Prepare!" The significance of this unusual message became clear through the events that followed.

As 1979 rolled on the desire to return to pastoral ministry grew and grew. October came and with it the call to pastor a church in Pickering,

Ontario, a growing community just east of Toronto. We were delighted and found great fulfillment in accepting the invitation of the board and congregation.

The desire for Israel continued to grow. We even thought of taking our daughters there for a trip, but we were not sure whether this was the Lord's idea or a personal dream. Privately, I had set the summer of 1980 as a target date for our trip. I pursued the possibility of a trip to Israel until February of 1980 when I made up my mind to drop the whole matter until I had a clear word from the Lord.

One morning, as I was praying, I said, "Lord, if you want us to go to Israel, then show us in a clear way so that we cannot mistake it to be Your will." That morning I got a call from one of the members of our congregation asking if our family would like to come for lunch. We were delighted to accept. Albert loved to cook and we loved to be with him and his family. During the course of the meal, Albert made a rather bold statement. He looked up and said, "You're going to Israel this year!" I looked at Marion and she looked at me. Without a word, each knew instinctively what the other was thinking: "How does he know about our desire to go to Israel?" We had not mentioned the possibility of a trip to Israel to anyone. We both began to laugh nervously. I asked, "What do you mean, brother?"

"The Lord has shown me that you're going to Israel," he replied. This opened the door for us to share our desire to visit the Holy Land. But God had another surprise for us that day. As we were leaving, Albert turned to me and said, "Not only are you going to Israel this year, but

I'm going to cover the cost of your accommodation."

After this the details of the trip began to fall into place. The Holy Spirit was faithful, nevertheless, to remind me that one detail was missing. We had the witness of God's Spirit through the dream of May, 1978. We had the witness through circumstance with Albert's generous offer, but we still needed a word from the Scriptures. As I was praying about this on Tuesday, May 13, just days before we were to leave for Israel, a thought came to mind. I remembered a good friend who, after completing his regular devotions, sometimes prays, "Lord, if You have something extra special today that I didn't receive in my daily passages, please speak to me now as I open my Bible." So I opened my Bible and placed my finger on the page at random. It fell upon Ezekiel 2:3, "And He said unto me, Son of Man, I send thee to the children of Israel..." (KJV). Without one flutter of emotion, I looked up and said, "Thank You Father, You speak very clearly." This was the final word of clearance. We knew God's peace and we were thankful.[2]

Israel was a spiritual treat. It was also a spiritual retreat. We were getting back to our spiritual roots. We were fascinated to observe the ancient and modern flowing together side by side. We stood by the Temple Mount, and thought of Abraham as we looked on the site of the greatest spiritual test of his life (Genesis 22:1-18). We visited a modern department store located in a skyscraper on King George V Street to purchase gifts for our daughters. We sat and meditated on our Lord's Resurrection in the peace and tranquility just outside the Garden

Tomb only yards away from the busy streets of Jerusalem. We investigated Hezekiah's tunnel, hewn out of the living rock seven centuries before Christ in order to provide a protected water supply to the city in time of seige (2 Kings 20:20). In modern Israel we saw that water is still a precious commodity as we noted the extensive systems of irrigation throughout the land.

Most of our time was spent in Jerusalem and we soon fell in love with the city and its people. The Lord had three significant events planned for us while there. The first event related to Jay and Meridel Rawlings who at the time were representatives for "100 Huntley Street" in Israel. Their job was to report on significant events in the Middle East. Marion and I had met Jay and Meridel while working at "100 Huntley Street" through mutual friends, Bruce and Moira Allan. Jay and Meridel's love for the Jewish people around the world had impressed us deeply. When they learned we were planning a trip to Israel, they invited us to drop in to their home in Jerusalem for a visit. We had their telephone number but no address so when we arrived, we made it a priority to get in touch. After several attempts to reach them, we dropped the matter thinking that they were out of town.

Then one afternoon we decided to enter the Old City of Jerusalem through the Jaffa Gate. From there, we walked to the south end and explored the Zion Gate. We had no sooner passed throught the gate, when I caught sight of Jay and his son in the distance. I shouted to get their attention as we walked toward them. I could not believe we had found him. Jay invited us back to their apartment in the Jewish Quarter of the Old City for a cup of tea. What a treat!

As we talked, one thing led to another until I was making plans to join Jay for early morning prayer. Our hearts were one in praying for Jerusalem and for Israel.

On June 2, we began what turned out to be eight early morning seasons of prayer. We spent the first morning at the Western or Wailing Wall, the remains of a wall that supported the platform where Solomon's Temple stood. Since the recapture of the Old City by Israel in 1967, this has been a sacred place of prayer for Jews from around the world. It was a deeply stirring experience for me. The next day, while in prayer with Jay, the Lord began to burden me for a program between people in Israel and Canada.

The second significant event occurred the following morning as I was walking down the Nablus Road from our hotel to the Old City. I was meditating on the events of the previous day. Over and over I found myself in conversation with the Lord about a Canadian prayer partner or worker who could help me build a bridge between Jewish and Christian people and between Canada and Israel. I was meditating on this when I caught sight of a mailbox. I had no letter to mail, but just as Moses was drawn to the burning bush, I had to investigate that box. It was set back into a stone wall. As I stood there examining the mailbox, my attention was drawn to the lower right hand corner where a small piece of plastic had been jammed in the crevice between the box and the wall. I reached in to pull out the piece of plastic only to discover that it was a strip of 35 mm film. As I held it up to the light, my heart began to pound as I read the name that appeared on each of the four frames. It was the same friend who had given me the word, "Prepare" back in April of 1979.

I had not seen this friend for over a year and so I prayed, "Lord, if You want us to be in touch, then You work it out." We arrived home from Israel on June 18, 1980. Guess who called two days later? It was a long distance call from Quebec. Since we had moved to Pickering some time before, calls were no longer automatically referred to our new number. One call had lead to another and it appeared there was a dead end. In the process of one last attempt, our friend asked the operator, "Could you give me the listing for Pastor Clyde Williamson?" The operator replied, "Oh, I know Clyde Williamson. He is in the South Pickering directory. I'll give you the number."

An official with Bell Canada has estimated that at any given time in a city the size of Toronto with a population of three million there are perhaps 4,000 telephone operators on duty. Add to this the fact that if the Toronto lines are particularly busy, your call for information could easily be shifted to an operator in another city who is free, say Ottawa, for example. This means that the chances of reaching one particular operator are quite slim. Add to this the chances of one of 4,000 people in a city of three million actually knowing the person you are searching for, and where they have moved recently, and you will realize who had His hand upon the Toronto telephone circuits that day.

The third significant event in Israel happened on June 5. I had recently been reading Nehemiah as well as several passages concerning both the feasts of Israel and the events of the end times. One passage in particular had stood out to me concerning the Feast of Tabernacles. It is found in Zechariah 14:16-18,

> In the end, those who survive the plague will go up to Jerusalem each year to worship the King, the Lord of Hosts, to celebrate a time of thanksgiving. And any nation anywhere in all the world that refuses to come to Jerusalem to worship the King, the Lord of Hosts, will have no rain. But if Egypt refuses to come, God will punish her with some other plague. And so Egypt and the other nations will all be punished if they refuse to come.
>
> (The Living Bible)

The way the Scriptures stated it left no question in my mind that the Feast of Tabernacles would be celebrated in the last days. As Jay and I began to pray that morning, all I could think about was this marvellous feast that God was going to cause His people to celebrate. During prayer I began to sense that I was to speak forth an utterance about the Feast of Tabernacles. According to the Scriptures it was to be celebrated. God would bring it to pass in His own time. Christian believers were to celebrate the feast as a preview to its celebration by the nations following the return of Jesus Christ at the end of the age. Boldly I declared this out loud, understanding it to be a word of knowledge from the Lord according to 1 Corinthians 12:8.[3]

Jay was silent. I thought he was upset at my boldness. I wondered if I was out of order. He said nothing until we descended from his rooftop a few flights of stairs and entered the apartment. We ended up in the kitchen. Jay looked at me with a strange expression on his face. Reaching forward to a bundle of papers on the counter, he pulled one out and handed it to me.

"Have you ever read this pamphlet on the

1979 Feast of Tabernacles?", he asked.

"No," I replied, "I didn't know there was a Feast of Tabernacles. That's exciting."

"Well," said Jay, "You have just spoken forth almost everything on that paper. We have been waiting on the Lord," he continued, "for confirmation to know if it is God's will for us to celebrate the Feast of Tabernacles again this year. You have just brought forth the word of encouragement that we needed. I'm going to call Merve and Merla Watson right away and let them know what has happened."

In the days that followed, Marion and I had some soul searching conversations on Israel. We always came to the same conclusion: It was not yet the Lord's time. To this I would always add, "But when, Lord?"

During the summer and fall of 1980, in my spare moments, I concentrated on reading books like, *The Death and Resurrection of Israel* by Arthur W. Kac. Understanding this resurrection was uppermost on my list of priorities. During this period, we were having weeks of special meetings in our church. I got so busy and tired that I ended up in bed most of October and November. The board and congregation were most understanding and stood with us through the whole ordeal. I made several visits to the doctor to determine the cause of the problem. At first he suspected heart trouble, but finally, he concluded it was simply exhaustion.

In the midst of all this the Lord Jesus, the great teacher, was speaking to me from Zechariah 4:6, "Not by might, nor by power, but by my Spirit, saith the Lord" (KJV). If there was going to be a resurrection of Israel, it would only come by the power of the Holy Spirit. If there was to be a resurrectrion of Clyde Williamson, it had to be by the same power. In this state of helplessness, lying on my bed alone for two months with my whole life's calling on the line, I learned one of the greatest lessons of my life. God's works have to be accomplished by God's power and in His strength.

In July, 1981, I was invited by an old friend, Pastor Al Bowen of Quebec City, to take a series of special meetings. I can remember the joy I experienced at being the first guest in his home to use what he and his wife Rene had christened, "the prophet's chamber". While out for a walk one night north of the Bowen's home, I asked the Lord if He had anything special to say to the first guest in "the prophet's chamber". With my French Bible in hand, I opened at random as I had done in mid-May of 1980. My eyes fell upon 1 Kings 17:3, "Get thee hence, and turn thee eastward, and hide thyself by the brook Cherith, that is before Jordan" (KJV). It was at this moment that the Spirit of God spoke to me about the word, "Kerith" (NIV) or "Cherith" (KJV). This verse was so significant that I thought for sure the Holy Spirit was directing me to move to Quebec City.

I thank God to this day that I was surrounded by understanding brothers who prayed the matter through with me. One of these was Pastor Don Krohn. Don had a word for me which I recorded in my diary, but have not read again until I began to write this book. We were in prayer when Don suddenly lifted his head and said, "I see you, Clyde, in a desert with a stream coming out of your mouth. You are planting

18

flowers in the desert and they are beginning to bloom." In those days Israel was something I thought about in my leisure hours which were few and far between. Don's statement seemed so deeply set in the context of Quebec City, that I completely missed its obvious message about Israel (see for example, Isaiah 35:1).

As we approached the fall of 1981, neither Marion or I could understand our feelings about Israel or about our church in Pickering. What did God have in mind? Such marvellous things were happening in the supernatural realm that pointed us toward a ministry to Israel. But in the natural realm, the doors seemed to be closing. As we waited upon the Lord, the only message we received was, "Hold steady."

While we were in this holding pattern, the Lord spoke supernaturally on three different occasions. The most significant of these was on January 5, 1982. I was praying with two men from our congregation in the Pickering church auditorium. It was 4:30 in the afternoon. As I was walking about, within my heart, I heard the Lord speak distinctly, "I'm going to speak to you at five minutes to five." I said nothing to my brethren, but went to stand under the clock at the back of the church at about six minutes to five. I was going to watch and wait. If I had heard from God, then God would speak. I watched the second hand of the clock sweep towards five to five. Ten seconds, nine, eight... four, three, two, one. At five to five, on the nose, the telephone rang. At first I thought it was the enemy trying to distract me from a vision or whatever the Lord had prepared for me. Then I realized that God could be speaking through the telephone by a messenger. I ran to the telephone and picked it up. The voice was a familiar one. It was my special Canada-Israel prayer partner who had said: "Clyde, prepare." This friend had been in a business meeting but was compelled to leave the meeting and call me. One call had been made and the line had gone dead. The second call got through. This friend began to exhort me in the Holy Spirit that God was bringing forth life. The message was about a new birth, a double anointing, and holiness. This message was confirmed exactly five and then ten days later by two totally unrelated people who could not have known the significance of what they were sharing with me. God was preparing our hearts for something very special.

Back to the situation in Pickering. About midnight on February 1, 1982 I had a clear sense in my heart that God was releasing us from our pastorate. The next morning as I awoke there was a fervent desire to call Pastor Ralph Rutledge of the Queensway Cathedral in Toronto. Over the years I had made periodic telephone calls to him when I felt the need of special prayer and direction from the Lord. What followed was unreal. The next day was February 2, the twentieth anniversary of my call to the Christian ministry. Early that morning, I called Pastor Rutledge. He invited me to a morning prayer meeting which I attended. I was there for his prayers, but I ended up being given a word for him. I knew he must read Daniel chapters 9 and 10. As it turned out, this passage was a strong confirmation to him about a decision he was facing. As the prayer time ended, I felt compelled to ask

Pastor Rutledge to go to lunch. He accepted and asked me if I would care to walk through the building with him to see some new offices. I followed feeling somewhat impatient to get this pastor to a place where I could talk to him privately. As we passed one of the new offices, he turned to me with a smile and said, "How would you like this office here as your new office?"

"What did you say?", I stammered. "Run that by me again!"

Before that lunch was over, I had answered every question he could throw my way about a position as Minister of Pastoral Care at Queensway Cathedral. Within the hour I called Marion with the prospect of coming to Queensway. One week later the call was confirmed. We began our ministry there on Sunday, March 21, 1982.

Footnotes:

1. *Most Roman Catholic translations use the numbering system for the Psalms found in the ancient Greek and Latin versions of the Old Testament. In all these versions, Psalms 9 and 10 are joined as well as Psalms 114 and 115, while Psalm 116 is divided into two as is Psalm 147. This means that Psalm 122:6 in the King James Version is Psalm 121:6 in most Roman Catholic Bibles.*

2. *As a Pastor, I feel constrained to point out that this should not be a regular method of spiritual guidance. I have used it perhaps a dozen times in my entire life. I had felt impressed that morning in prayer that God wanted to speak to me through His Word. My practice has been, if the verse chosen makes sense, if there is a quickening of the Holy Spirit, and if it lines up with other methods of guidance, I accept it. If it makes no sense, I forget it.*

3. *"For to one is given by the Spirit the word of wisdom; to another the word of knowledge by the same Spirit" (1 Corinthians 12:8, KJV). Biblical examples of this phenomena of supernaturally revealed information include Jesus' insight into the domestic situation of the woman at the well (John 4:16-19) and Peter's knowledge that Ananias and Sapphira were lying (Acts 5:1-10).*

CHAPTER TWO

Caught by the Wind

Queensway Cathedral in Toronto, is the home of the weekly telecast, "Revival Hour." Pastor Ralph Rutledge, the senior pastor at Queensway has, as do I, a burning desire to see God's will for the nation of Canada fulfilled. During my first year on the pastoral staff at Queensway, it was "the Lord's business as usual" until God spoke to Pastor Rutledge on Sunday, January 2, 1983. He was deeply impressed of the Holy Spirit to extend an invitation to the entire congregation to join in a forty-day fast. Those who personally sensed the same call were encouraged to participate. The fast was called for the period from Monday, January 10 through Friday, February 18, 1983. It was to be concluded with a solemn assembly on Sunday, February 20.

During the morning service that first Sunday in January, Pastor Rutledge declared that it was time for the Church to Awake, Alert, and Advance. The Church must Awake to who God is in holiness. She must heed the Alert by setting the stage for the supernatural. She must prepare to Advance by seeking to become a people prepared for the Lord. These three themes were understood as the response God desired from His people to the call delivered through Pastor

Rutledge exactly a year before in January, 1982. Three times he had been awakened in the night with Joel 2:1, "Blow ye the trumpet in Zion, and sound an alarm in my holy mountain" (KJV).

The Sunday following the call to the forty-day fast, January 7, 1983, once again Pastor Rutledge felt impressed of the Lord to "Blow the trumpet in Zion." This was understood as a confirmation of the call to fasting and prayer delivered the previous Sunday. The fast was the key to heeding the call to Awake, Alert, and Advance since it could only be through repentance that the necessary restoration and refreshing would come. God was calling upon His people to surrender to Him in a fuller measure and thus to enter into a new relationship of trust in Him and dependance upon Him.

I was prompted by the Holy Spirit to begin this forty-day fast with an Esther Fast. This meant not eating or drinking for three days and three nights (Esther 4:16). I felt at this time such a burden for revival in Canada. Ever since I was filled with the Holy Spirit at Easter, in 1963, this has been the cry of my heart. Canada needed a national-wide revival, a sovereign move of God that would bring people by the thousands into an experience of repentance followed by righteous living. I wanted to be available for God to use me in any way He chose to bring this about. Along with many others across the nation, I was desperate for God to give revival to Canada.

On the fourteenth day of the forty-day fast, Sunday, January 23, I felt deep groanings of intercession during the afternoon hours alone in prayer at home. In my mind and spirit I was experiencing a panoramic review of all that the Lord had shown me concerning Israel over the

24

years. In this way, God was preparing me for what was about to transpire during the 6:00 p.m. service that same evening.

The focus of the service was the nation of Israel, the people of God. The guest speaker was Jan Willem van der Hoeven, of the International Christian Embassy in Jerusalem. Special music was provided by Merve and Merla Watson, a couple who have ministered to the Jewish people for years and who also live in Jerusalem. Following a word of exhortation from Pastor Rutledge, Brother van der Hoeven stepped forward to minister God's Word. He declared that Canada would be blessed only as she would bless Israel (Genesis 12:3). God was looking for intercessors to stand in the gap and make up the hedge for the land of Israel (Ezekiel 22:30). Would He find them in our assembly? His message set my heart pounding. Following the sermon, Pastor Rutledge said a few words and then invited Merve and Merla Watson to sing in worship unto the Lord. The sense of God's presence filled the sanctuary. When they had finished singing, I knew I must speak. As I stepped to the pulpit, a word of exhortation came forth out of my mouth that was destined to go around the world, the word concerning the Esther Fast. The congregation received this as a word of exhortation from the Lord. Our hearts were stirred!

The next evening, Monday, January 24, I was at home in the kitchen eating on one of my forty-day fast evening "meals." As I was munching on crackers and drinking a cup of warm water, I began to reflect on a particular part of the Sunday evening exhortation on the Esther Fast: "And God shall give an appointed time...."

"What is to be the date of this fast, Lord?" I

prayed. As if I was in a conversation, the Lord replied with great clarity in my spirit, "April 1, 2, and 3." I quickly flipped over our kitchen calendar only to discover to my amazement that these dates fell on Good Friday, Holy Saturday, and Easter Sunday. "What timing!" I exclaimed out loud. Ecstatic with joy, I had to tell Marion! Leaping two and three stairs at a time, I rushed upstairs and bounded into the family room where my wife was sitting.

"Darling, guess what?"

"Now calm down, dear. Take it easy," was her reply. "What's got you all excited?" she asked.

I quickly related to her my prayer and the very significant dates the Lord had just given to me. Her response was to jump up and start looking for a calendar we had with all the Jewish holidays marked on it. To our amazement the Eshter Fast not only fell on Easter weekend, but it also came right in the middle of the Jewish Passover! It seemed that whatever God's plans were, this fast had a double anointing on it. Surely we were to pray for both Jewish and Christian people. Glory to God!

The next day, Jacques Gauthier, one of our elders came to me with a strong word of encouragement to pursue in obedience what the Holy Spirit had exhorted us to do. He reasoned, "If God is speaking, then we better do something about it." This word of encouragement ignited afresh the message of the Esther Fast in my heart and brought me to the place of prayer. In a very short time, God was going to show us that He desired the word of the Esther Fast to be proclaimed literally around the globe.

Friday evening, January 28, I was at the church

late following the meeting of the New Life Fellowship, Queensway's small-group discipleship program. I left the office to go home but felt led to return. I was not more than a few minutes back in the office when Stan Watrich, another of our elders, dropped in to say hello. He had a scripture related to the events of the week that he wanted to share with me from Isaiah 52:5-10,

> Now therefore, what have I here, saith the Lord, that my people is taken away for nought? They that rule over them make them to howl, saith the Lord; and my name continually every day is blasphemed. Therefore my people shall know my name: therefore they shall know in that day that I am he that doth speak: behold, it is I. How beautiful upon the mountains are the feet of him that bringeth good tidings, that publisheth peace; that bringeth good tidings of good, that publisheth salvation; that saith unto Zion, Thy God reigneth! Thy watchmen shall lift up the voice; with the voice together shall they sing: for they shall see eye to eye, when the Lord shall bring again Zion. *The watchmen shout and sing with joy, for right before their eyes they see the Lord God bring His people home again. Break forth into joy, sing together, ye waste places of Jerusalem: for the Lord hath comforted his people, he hath redeemed Jerusalem. The Lord hath made bare his holy arm in the eyes of all the nations; and all the ends of the earth shall see the salvation of our God.

(*KJV, verse 8 is repeated from The Living Bible)

This Scripture portion so stirred me that I decided to take home a copy of the tape recording of the evening service during which I had spoken the message concerning the Esther Fast the week before. In listening to the tape, I found this exhortation so challenging that I copied it out word for word.

It is important to note at this point that I have

no desire to set prophetic utterances or public messages of exhortation alongside the Scriptures as possessing equal authority. In fact, such a practice is logically impossible since we are called upon to judge every prophetic utterance on the basis of Scriptural teaching (1 Corinthians 14:29). Anything that counsels us to set aside God's truth is to be rejected (Deuteronomy 13:1-6). My desire simply is to be obedient to the prompting of the Holy Spirit in my life even as Peter was when he obeyed the Spirit's guidance through the vision of the sheet full of unclean animals and proceeded to preach the gospel to the Gentiles (Acts 10:9-11:12).

I have discovered that I rarely grasp the significance of God's supernatural leading in my life at the time it occurs. It is only with much prayer and reflection that I see the intention of these experiences when I face a new situation that sheds light on what God has been speaking to me all along. Only then am I at liberty to take the next step along the path that lies ahead. In this way, I allow the Holy Spirit Himself to make clear the significance of a particular experience which, in itself, could give rise to all sorts of interpretations based upon my own speculations.

It is with these remarks in mind that I present a summary of the word of exhortation concerning the Esther Fast given on January 23, 1983, at Queensway Cathedral:

The Spirit of the Lord shall bring forth a mighty work in your hearts. For you have by the Spirit of the Lord heard His voice calling you to pray for the people of Israel. And you have stepped forth into that arena of intercession to which the Spirit of the living God has called you. For indeed everywhere across this auditorium and across this nation the Spirit of God is wooing people to do that which Queen Esther did in an absolute fast unto God, a fast in which to seek God for the restoration and deliverance of the people of Israel.

And God shall give an appointed time and there shall be those in His body that shall set themselves aside without food and without drink for a period of three days that God will set forth out of bondage, His people (both Israel and the Church) from all over the globe. And they shall come forth by the thousands and by the millions and His name shall be glorified.

This is a challenge that the Spirit of God is giving to this nation, the nation of Canada. The Church of Canada shall lead the way and challenge not only her own nation, but the world to bow at the feet of Jesus and to cry unto the Lord, that the people of God worldwide be set free to fulfill their mission of blessing to all the families of the earth.

And as we are attentive unto His voice, He will provide an open path before us. It will not be easy. There will be battles! There will be at times confusion, but they that wait upon the Lord shall understand the will of God. And, they will go forth in battle, for indeed it shall be the beginning of an unleashing of great powers, powers of righteousness and also of darkness. For surely the Spirit of the Lord shall bring forth that which He desires to accomplish on behalf of His people.

As I awoke that Saturday morning, following my talk with Stan Watrich the night before, all I could think about was that the Esther Fast had to be announced publicly everywhere. The regular events of life occupied my attention until I received a call that afternoon from Pastor Rutledge. He wanted to go over the events of the week in preparation for Sunday. As an aside in our conversation, I asked if he had any sense of direction about what we were to do regarding the Esther Fast. He suggested that I put some ideas together and drop over to his home that evening at 8 p.m. We would spend fifteen minutes together.

That fifteen minutes turned into three hours. As we began to share about what to do concerning the Esther Fast, the Pastor decided to run the idea past his brother-in-law, David Mainse, President of "100 Huntley Street," Canada's daily Christian telecast. At the time David was attending the National Religious Broadcasters conference in Washington, D.C. While we were considering calling David Mainse, who should phone but his wife, Norma Jean, who is Pastor Rutledge's sister. She was calling from her home in Toronto to give Ralph an update on how things were going at the conference, having just spoken with David in Washington.

Ralph shared with her what was happening regarding the Esther Fast and asked for David's telephone number in Washington. Pastor Rutledge then called David while I listened on an extension. David was ecstatic about the idea of publishing the announcement, objectives, and dates of the Esther Fast at the conference there in Washington.

"David believes it's the Lord!" Pastor kept saying in a loud whisper pointing to the phone with excitement in his eyes.

Up to this point, Pastor Rutledge had held back from attending the NRB conference. Although he was entitled to be there as the host of "Revival Hour," as usual, he wanted to stay close by his flock. But now things had changed. He had an important mission to accomplish. He would go to the conference and do all he could to proclaim the call to the Esther Fast. While still on the phone with David Mainse, he asked me to call the airline and book his flight which I did. He was to leave on Monday morning, January 31.

Something had to be done to get the details of the Esther Fast down on paper. It was now already Saturday night. Immediately, we called Stan Watrich who owns a printing firm to ask if an Esther Fast proclamation could by typeset and printed in time to leave for Washington Monday morning at 10:30 a.m. Stan said it could be done although he would have to bring in some of his people on Sunday and pay them overtime.

It was down to the wire. There were many things to decide. Do we put the name of our church on the proclamation or leave it off? We did not want any credit for what God was doing. What was the proper thing to do? Jacques Gauthier, the elder who had been so helpful at the outset of the week who is a lawyer, was invited to help with the wording of the proclamation. We decided it should look like a scroll. As we all shared back and forth it was agreed that the name of the church should be put on the scroll just as a signature is applied to a document to give it authenticity. The wind of the Holy Spirit had caught hold of the scroll and would send its message far and wide!

When Pastor Rutledge arrived in Washington, David Mainse was quick to share with him how he had already spoken of the Esther Fast to a Jewish gentleman. The man had responded by saying he was "dumbfounded that Christians would have anything to do with Jewish people in a fast of this nature."

David also said that he was producing a special telecast that evening in Washington which would be released from Toronto all across Canada and the United States first thing the next morning, February 1. His guests would be Jim Bakker of the PTL Network, Rex Humbard, John Wesley White of the Billy Graham Evangelistic Association, and Jerry Rose of Channel 38 in Chicago. He also invited Ralph to join in the telecast. How amazing is the timing of God. The scroll was only twenty-four hours off the press and already news of it was being released across both Canada and the United States on television.

During their brief stay in Washington, David and Ralph managed to speak with several others about the Esther Fast including Pat Robertson of the 700 Club; Demos Shekarian, International President of the Full Gospel Business Men's Association; Cliff Barrows of the Billy Graham team; and Dr. Thomas Zimmerman, General Superintendent of the Assemblies of God.

The highlight of that Monday evening telecast was an insert taken from President Ronald Reagan's address to the NRB conference earlier that day. The President began by declaring, "The American people are hungry for your message (that of religious broadcasters) because they are hungry for a spiritual revival in this land."

A little later in his address he added, "We want to face the future with the Bible. You might be happy to hear," he continued, "that I have some good news of my own. Thursday morning (February 3, 1983) at the National Prayer Breakfast, I will sign a proclamation making 1983, 'The Year of the Bible'." These were encouraging words from the highest elected official in

America. What President Reagan had to say at the conclusion of his speech, however, was truly amazing when you consider it became part of a program to promote the Esther Fast for the release and restoration of God's people:

I know that each of you is contributing in your own way to rebuilding America and I thank you. As broadcasters you have unique opportunities and all of us as Protestants, Catholics, and Jews have a special responsibility to remember our fellow believers who are being persecuted in other lands. We're all children of Abraham. We're children of the same God. Alexander Herzen, the Russian writer has warned: "To shrink from saying a word in defense of the oppressed is as bad as any crime." Well, I pledge to you that America will stand up, speak out, and defend the values we share. To those who would crush religious freedom our message is plain: You may jail your believers, you may close their churches, confiscate their Bibles and harass their rabbis and priests, but you will never destroy the love of God and freedom in their hearts. They will triumph over you!

God was indeed calling for just such a word to be spoken in defense of the oppressed, but it was not to be a word of protest conveyed through diplomatic channels to an oppressive power. It was to be a mighty voice of intercession crying out to God to give release for the captives, both physical and spiritual release that His purposes might be accomplished and that His name alone might be glorified in the earth.

On the same day that President Reagan proclaimed 1983, "The Year of the Bible", he met with members of the World Jewish Congress in the White House. His remarks were directed against what he considered to be the violent anti-Semitic policies of the Soviet government.

The president said that Jews face adversity in the Soviet Union, are denied basic rights to study and practice their religion, and are subjected to "brutal harassment" if they want to emigrate. As he had declared at the NRB conference, so he declared to the World Jewish Congress members, "We will not forget them." He called upon the Soviets to release the prisoners of conscience in Siberia and restore Jewish emigration to the levels of the late 1970's.

God was beginning to fuel the fires of intercession in our hearts. I began to sense the compassion of our Saviour as He wept over His beloved chosen ones crying out, "O Jerusalem, Jerusalem..." (Luke 13:34). I knew instinctively that this marked the end of one chapter in my life and the beginning of another.

CHAPTER THREE

A Matter of Life and Death

The video tape of the "100 Huntley Street" telecast made in Washington, D.C. on Monday, January 31, was flown to the Canadian studio for release across Canada the next morning over the Global Television Network. It included the discussion of the Esther Fast and President Reagan's address to the NRB conference. Simultaneously it was being released across the United States over the PTL Network. The word of the Esther Fast was exploding forth. While this miracle of the Holy Spirit and of modern technology was happening, I was in my office at Queensway Cathedral in prayer seeking God for the message He wanted me to share at the Tuesday mid-week service I was taking that evening in Pastor Rutledge's absence.

During that period of preparation I got a call saying that President Reagan's entire address was available on audio tape through "100 Huntley Street." Arrangements were made immediately to get a copy of the tape. I knew that the highlights of the President's message had to be part of the service that night. Having stepped out in obedience to the Holy Spirit, we were now watching God work miracles on every hand. I had a keen sense that we were advancing rapidly on the crest of a wave sent by the Lord.

As 7:30 p.m. approached on that Tuesday evening, my heart was in my mouth. I did not know what I should talk about. In the first part of the service, Pastor Kenn Gill led a powerful introduction emphasizing the theme of faith in the songs that were sung and the scriptures he shared. He then turned the service over to me.

As I began to speak, the ushers handed out a copy of the Esther Fast scroll to each person present. I shared with the people how the message of the scroll had been taken to Washington and presented by Pastor Rutledge at the NRB conference. Although some of the congregation had seen the special program that morning on "100 Huntley Street," most were unaware that it was being released simultaneously across the United States. A moment later, to everyone's surprise and delight, they were listening to a portion of President Reagan's NRB address which I had arranged to be played over the public address system. The congregation began to catch the spirit of the conference that was still going on in Washington at that very moment. This was where the Holy Spirit had chosen to release the news concerning the Esther Fast. Everyone was excited.

A spirit of boldness gripped me: "God is going to open doors into governments in the next few hours and days," I declared. I then turned to Ezekiel 22:30 and read,

> I looked up for a man among them who would build up the wall and stand before me in the gap on behalf of the land so I would not have to destroy it, but I found none.

I proclaimed that now is the time to weep and cry unto God just as the people of Ninevah did in Jonah's day (Jonah 3:6-10). I then read the words of Jonah 3:7 where the king issues a decree: "Do not let any man or beast, herd or flock, taste anything; do not let them eat or drink." What a desperate cry! The king and all the people believed Jonah's warning and obeyed it. The words: "Do not let them eat or drink" were the very call of the Esther Fast (Esther 4:16). "This fast is not to be a burden," I declared, "but something to be done joyfully, something born in the Holy Spirit, something you want to do with all your heart."

By now my own heart was bursting: "We have come to this day, we have come to this time, 'Let everyone call urgently on God!' (Jonah 3:8) This is national and international warfare on our knees! We are in a battle, commissioned by the God of heaven to strike around the world!"

After this I mentioned that Dr. Paul Yonggi Cho had declared with no uncertainty that Canada could become a mighty nation of prayer that would shake the world for God. It was burning in my heart to send him a copy of the Esther Fast scroll. Near the end of my message, I directed the congregation to Jeremiah 16:14-16,

"However, the days are coming," declares the Lord, "when men will no longer say, 'As surely as the Lord lives, who brought the Israelites up out of Egypt,' but they will say 'As surely as the Lord lives, who brought the Israelites up out of the land of the north and out of all the countries where he had banished them.' For I will restore them to the land I gave their forefathers.

"But now I will send for many fishermen," declares the Lord, "and they will catch them. After that I will send for many hunters, and they will hunt them down on every mountain and hill and from the crevices of the rocks."

I explained it was the responsibility of believers everywhere to pray for the Jewish people that they might understand God's call and be part of this mighty release from the north (Russia) and other nations where they dwell. Further, we were to be as "fishermen" and extend an invitation to every Jewish person we met to go up to live in Israel before the "hunters" would come. I commented that there is an excellent explanation of this call to Israel worldwide in Jay and Meridel Rawling's book entitled, *Fishers and Hunters*.[1]

I concluded by saying, "The pronouncement of a national fast is a rare and significant event in the Word of God. God is not playing games. This is *a matter of life and death for Israel*." I explained that the purpose of the Esther Fast is the same as it was in the days of Queen Esther, to save the people of Israel from annihalation. According to Isaiah 52:5-10, the good news of God's salvation will be proclaimed to Israel so that all the world may see the glory of God. God is going to fulfill His Word on behalf of Israel. I pointed out that we have the opportunity of joining in prayer and fasting. If we will travail in intercession along with Israel here and around the world, God's Holy Spirit will bring Zion forth in a day in the spiritual, just as He brought her forth in a day in the natural on May 14, 1948, when the State of Israel was born.[2]

I closed the service with a challenge to this mid-week group of 800 to 900 people to take as many copies of the scroll as they could use and prayerfully distribute them to people they knew. They were directed to mail them to believers in Toronto, throughout Canada, and around the world.

In a few moments Maggie Larmand rushed up to me full of excitement. She wanted to know if I would be willing to speak to her father, Donald Morand. Mr. Morand was the Ombudsman of Ontario and had personal contacts with government officials all over the world. Maggie would be willing to ask his permission to send scrolls out to all of these officials. The match had been struck! People all over the auditorium were on fire with the worldwide call to fast and pray for the Release, Return, Restoration and Revival of both Israel and the Church of Jesus Christ.

The next morning, February 2, I plunged into my daily devotions with a thirst for God like I'd never known. My passage for that day was Isaiah, chapter 59. As I studied it, all I could think of was Daniel confessing his sins and the sins of his nation (Daniel, chapter 9). The cry of intercession again gripped my heart. In reflecting on the service of the night before, I had never imagined that the groanings of the Holy Spirit could be so deep in my spirit.

Following staff devotions that morning at church, I asked Don Morrow, our Minister of Christian Education, to join me in a special time of prayer. As we prayed, we sensed God was calling us to a new walk of self-denial. In my heart, God was whispering that He desired a profound change in me, Clyde Williamson. These thoughts were so significant, that I wrote them down and shared them later with Pastor Rutledge and the staff. I knew something was different. A new stage of my life was unfolding. I had been ushered into a new place in God.

Later that morning in my office, Susan Poole, our Pastoral Care Secretary, informed me that

39

my mother had called and I should call her right back. Over the years my mother has been a faithful prayer partner to me. I dialed my parent's number and my mother answered. Her voice betrayed her excitement.

"Clyde," she said, "I have a passage that the Lord wants me to give to you. Have you got a pencil and paper?"

"Yes, go ahead," I replied.

"Write down Isaiah 59:19-21. I believe it's especially for you today."

"Whoo!" I said in reply, "That's the very passage through which God spoke to me so clearly in my devotions this morning! Isn't that exciting!" I asked her to pray for the Lord to clarify the passage and the overall significance of what God was trying to say. She agreed and we said goodbye. What would the Lord do next?

Another call came, this time from Maggie Larmond following through on her commitment from the night before. She had been in touch with her father, Mr. Morand, and he had given permission for me to come to see him. Did not the Lord say in the service that He was going to open doors into governments?

No sooner had I hung up the phone than Susan was putting another call through. This time it was Pastor David Bowen. Brother Bowen, his wife Margaret, and their family had opened their hearts and their home to Marion and I when we first began dating. Down through the years we have seen wonderful things happen together as God has moved in our lives. One of these was the birth of a children's ministry out of Brother Bowen's church which eventually became Kamp Kuriou, a Christian ministry to underprivileged children. As I spoke with Brother

Bowen, I felt impressed to ask him if he would join me in visiting Donald Morand that afternoon. He was delighted.

We arrived at a prestigious looking building at the corner of University and Bloor in downtown Toronto for our 1:30 p.m. appointment. Mary, Mr. Morand's secretary was very cordial.

"Mr. Morand will be ready for you in just a few minutes. Would you please have a seat?"

The building where Mr. Morand's office was located was a magnificent piece of architecture. The high ceilings, the huge marble staircases and the immense rooms were all quite breathtaking. In a few moments we had entered Mr. Morand's office. After introducing himself he thanked Pastor Bowen and I for coming to share with him news of the Esther Fast. His daughter, Maggie, had explained a little about the fast, but he wanted more information. What was supposed to be a very brief visit turned out to be a leisurely time of getting acquainted. As Brother Bowen and I left, we sensed the warmth of God's presence and blessing upon us. Not only did we receive Mr. Morand's permission to send the scrolls to his contacts around the world, he also wished us God's blessing on our project.

As we stepped out into the street, Brother Bowen suggested that we visit the Ontario Parliament Buildings just down the street. Before we did this, however, I just happened to look up the street and see the word, "Israel." It was printed on the sign for the "Israel Discount Bank of Canada" at 150 Bloor Street West. We went to the bank and left several copies of the scroll with the management.

Once this was done, we returned to Brother Bowen's car and headed down University Avenue to the Parliament Buildings. We entered the Provincial Legislature and were making our way to the office of Premier William Davis to give him a copy of the scroll, when we noticed that *CFTO News*, a local T.V. station, was doing a taping. We stood and watched the crew at work while we waited to speak with one of the newspeople. Eventually we were able to speak with Christine Bently, a local newsperson, and tell her about the Esther Fast. Her attention had been captured when we mentioned we had a tape of President Reagan's address to the NRB conference in Washington given earlier that week. After a brief conversation, we gave her the tape, she thanked us, and we were on our way. This door did not open for T.V. coverage, but another did later. Both Pastor Rutledge and I were interviewed by Jeff Ansell of *City TV*. Part of this interview dealing with the Esther Fast was released on the regular 10 p.m. newscast.

The day was not over yet. That evening the Lord had a special surprise in store for me. Some months before I had received an invitation from Paul and Maureen Giroux to speak at the Upper Room on Yonge Street. This was a weekly inter-denominational Charismatic fellowship. It had been very difficult for me to decide upon a topic. The story was different now. My question was, "Would I have enough time to share all that was bursting in my mind and spirit?"

No sooner had I come through the door than Maureen came over and began enthusiastically to relate that she had just been talking to Meridel Rawlings in Jerusalem. Meridel had told her about the word of knowledge that had come forth at the Feast of Tabernacles in the fall of 1982 confirming that she and her husband Jay should go and stand in Moscow during Passover of 1983 and speak a word of release for the Jewish people in that land.

Paul and Maureen are a very special couple who have been part of the Charismatic movement in the Roman Catholic church. They are keenly interested in Israel and in the Jewish people. They did not know about the Esther Fast until I arrived that night. Neither did I know about the word of confirmation to Jay and Meridel regarding their trip to Moscow. As it all turned out, the news Maureen conveyed concerning the Rawlings was further confirmation of the timing of the Esther Fast. But that was not all. At the conclusion of the evening, after a very blessed time of ministry in which I shared the call to the Esther Fast, Maureen said, "I know Paul wouldn't share this, but I feel I must. He has just completed a three-day Esther Fast today!" It was not until weeks later after piecing all these events together, that I realized the significance of the timing of Maureen's remarks about the Rawlings' trip to Russia.

On Thursday, February 10, I sent a letter with the news about the Esther Fast and copies of the scroll to Jay and Meridel in Jerusalem. That same day, in Israel, Jay was writing out a bill to the Queensway for 200 copies of their book, *Fishers and Hunters*. This was enclosed with a letter dated February 16. As mail takes anywhere from two to three weeks to get from Canada to Israel, they would not have received my letter before they had sent their letter off to me. This is

43

evident from the contents of their letter.

As Jay related to me later, they had been in special prayer once again asking the Lord to confirm their step of faith in going to Moscow. They were waiting for that extra word from the Lord because of the nature of the mission. It was precisely at that time my letter arrived with the announcement of the Esther Fast for April 1, 2, and 3, 1983. Those were precisely the dates the Rawlings had planned for the trip to Moscow, the dates they were asking the Lord to confirm the day the Esther Fast scroll arrived!

But that is not the whole story. On Monday, March 7, I awoke with a burden to call Jay. It was 6:15 a.m. which meant that it would be 1:15 p.m. in Israel. My purpose in calling was to share several verses the Lord had given me for he and Meridel. These I had written into my pocket calendar the day before.

Here is what I shared with Jay over the telephone:

> Do not be afraid, for I am with you; I will bring your children from the east and gather you from the west. I will say to the north, "Give them up!" and to the south, "Do not hold them back." Bring my sons from afar and my daughters from the ends of the earth – everyone who is called by my name whom I created for my glory, whom I formed and made.
>
> (Isaiah 43:5-7)
>
> Go proclaim this message toward the north: "Return, faithless Israel," declares the Lord, "I will frown on you no longer, for I am merciful," declares the Lord, "I will not be angry forever."
>
> (Jeremiah 3:12)

At 3:55 p.m. on the afternoon of Wednesday, March 9, Pastor Rutledge's secretary, Jan brought me a copy of the Rawlings' prayer letter which had just arrived. The reason she did this was because of the announcement it contained about the Esther Fast. They had been quick to get the news out after receiving the scrolls. What Jan did not know was that in the same letter, Jay had quoted Isaiah 43:5-6 and requested prayer for their trip to Moscow. These were two of the five verses I had given to Jay only two days earlier by telephone. In other words, my call had simply confirmed what God had already spoken to Jay when he sent off the prayer letter a week or more before. It is evident that the Lord whispers over and over again when He wishes to confirm His perfect will and bring confidence to those who need His assurance.

As February 2 came to a close, so did the celebration of the twenty-first anniversary of my call to the Christian ministry. Praise to my Heavenly Father filled my heart. His call was more profound than ever. I was beginning to see very clearly that part of that call was related to praying for the release of the Jewish people not only from Russia, but from all over the world.

Footnotes:

1. See *Fishers and Hunters* by Jay and Meridel Rawlings, abridged edition, chapters 8, 12, and 21.

2. The concept conveyed in this paragraph relates to the true nature of prayer. Essentially, prayer is our co-operation with God in the fulfillment of His purposes in the earth. It could be argued that God does not need our

intercession to fulfill the prophecy of Isaiah 66:5-11 (cf.Zechariah chs.12-14) concerning the spiritual rebirth of Israel. And yet we cannot fail to note that God used the intercession of His people like Nehemiah (1:3-11) and Daniel (9:1-19) to restore Israel to the land following the Babylonian Captivity. We do not know for sure if Daniel ever lived to see the answer to his cry of intercession, and yet God recorded these things in His Word for our instruction. Whether we believe we will live to see the nation of Israel spiritually reborn in a day depends on our understanding of Bible prophecy. But the fact that we may not be here to see the fulfillment should not hinder us from heeding His call to intercession on behalf of Israel.

CHAPTER FOUR

God's News Travels Fast!

The months of February and March flew by. With extra telephone calls, interviews, mailings, and all the regular church activities as well as being on a forty-day fast, I found it quite a challange to spend proper time with my family.

A very siginficant meeting which actually took place in May following the fast helped me to understand the Jewish perspective on the Esther Fast. I turned to my wife Marion for help in setting up the meeting. Marion works part-time as a dental assistant to Dr. Arnie Shulman who attends the Beth Tikvah synagogue. I called Beth Tikvah and, using Dr. Shulman's name as a reference, explained who I was and requested a meeting with Rabbi Robert Marcus. He was willing to see me and so we set a time for the appointment.

When I arrived at the synagogue office, although the atmosphere was quite cordial, I sensed in Rabbi Marcus a certain cautiousness regarding the exact purpose of my visit. After we introduced ourselves, I commented on the natural suspicions Jewish and Christian people have for one another. He responded, "Well, we never know what to expect, you know." Sensing a hint of humour in his voice, I felt more relaxed and we began to chat freely.

After I had told him about the Esther Fast, he commented that Stan Solomon, one of Avital and Anatoly Shcharansky's relatives, was in his congregation. This was my introduction to the Shcharansky family. I also took it as a call to pray for this imprisoned Soviet Jewish dissident.

As we moved from the topic of Jewish refuseniks to Bible prophecy, I began to share my views on this subject with great excitement. When I had finished, Rabbi Marcus commented, "I don't mean to be unkind, but what I sense most is a Christian lack of understanding for the suffering of Jewish people, not only in the Holocaust and in Russia, but also in modern Israel. Your focus is on future victory while our focus must be on present tragedy." He then began to paint a panoramic picture of the suffering of so many in Israel following the Yom Kippur War of 1973. He described the number of families affected, the types of injuries suffered, and the tragic waste of human life. By the time he concluded, I found it difficult to speak. There was a lump in my throat. I had never learned these things from reading newspapers or books. To this day I thank the Lord for that visit. Now, every time I stand to speak on modern Israel, I sense in a small way the depth of agony of which Rabbi Marcus spoke.

The day-by-day events of how the word of the Esther Fast went forth are best shared in the form of a diary.

On February 1, following a service at Queensway Cathedral, Jacqueline, a Finnish lady, grabbed my arm and said enthusiastically, "People in Finland are storing food and clothing in preparation to receive Jewish people as they come out of Russia according to Jeremiah 23:7-8."

On February 2, Jan Willem van der Hoeven, spokesman for the the International Christian Embassy in Jerusalem wrote a letter that was forwarded to Alan Lazerte, Executive Director of the Canadian Friends of the International Christian Embassy. The letter's message was clear. It invited Christians everywhere to participate in Mordecai outcrys. These were to be held in front of Russian embassies all over the world. The cry was that this, "Pharaoh of the North" would, "Let God's people go."

The next day, on February 3, I shared with Pastor Rutledge the events of the meeting of the previous evening at the Upper Room with Paul and Maureen Giroux. One of the things that took place at the meeting concerned an invitation to fly to Switzerland to meet with Jacob Zopfi, the leader of the European Pentecostal Conference. I would then itinerate in various churches to proclaim the news of the Esther Fast. This trip did not materialize, but thanks to Walter Kast, who was in Toronto training at "100 Huntley Street" to open a television network in Switzerland, the Esther Fast information was personally conveyed to Mr. Zopfi. Jacob Zopfi sent copies of the scroll to church leaders in Denmark, Finland, Iceland, Norway, Sweden, Belgium, England, France, Austria, West Germany, Holland, Switzerland, Bulgaria, East Germany, Hungary, Poland, Romanaia, Yugoslavia, Greece, Italy, and Portugal – twenty-one nations!

That afternoon, Larseric Janson, Vice President of IBRA Radio in Stockholm dropped into my office in the midst of his very busy Canadian itineray to hear about the fast. This station reaches twenty million people in Europe on both sides of the Iron Curtain. Unfortunately, my correspondence to him which followed did not arrive in time for broadcast before the Esther Fast was held. This missed opportunity appears to have been overruled in that George Otis of High Adventure Ministries was able from his broadcasting tower in Lebanon to beam an announcement concerning the Esther Fast in short wave to Russia in mid-March.

More good news came later that afternoon. Ken Hoover of "100 Huntley Street" called regarding details on the reprinting of the Esther Fast scroll for distribution across Canada to the listening audience of this daily Christian television program.

On Sunday evening, February 6, requests for 399 scrolls came in by card from the Queensway congregation. These would be packaged and ready for distribution to those who had requested them on Tuesday, February 8. They were to be sent to other churches in Toronto, family and friends in various cities in Canada, as well as destinations abroad including Zambia, South Africa, Togo, Ghana, England, Australia, Guyana, Sweden, Jordan, Israel, Costa Rica, the U.S.A., Cyprus, Lebanon, Spain, Switzerland and Abu Dhabi. These scrolls were going out to both Jewish and Christian people in these countries.

By Tuesday, February 8, we realized we could not keep up with the requests for copies of the scroll and so we asked people to take one copy and photocopy or have printed the number they required. The Holy Spirit was doing the work.

All we had to do was be obedient and send the scrolls to every one we knew who believed in the power of prayer.

That same day by letter, Jacques Gauthier, the elder who helped us with the wording of the scroll, offered some further help. On its way at his expense from his office was a beautiful full-colour map of the world and a box of push pins to identify the cities and countries where the scrolls were being sent. The comment in his letter to me that day expressed what he, his wife Rani, and hundreds of others were sensing. He wrote, "I am so excited about what is unfolding before our eyes. Rani and I want so much to be a part of it."

By that evening, thanks to a couple of men in the church, the world map was mounted on a bulletin board in the auditorium. At the top they printed, "The Esther Fast, April 1, 2, and 3, 1983." To the left of this were the words, "Release and Return." To the right were the words, "Restoration and Revival." There was a place designated for total contacts to date. This was broken down into the number of cities/towns, nations, and Jewish contacts where the scrolls were being sent. Using an overhead projector during the service, we showed the congregation the countries of the world where the scrolls were being sent. Everyone was invited to pray over these countries and to continue mailing the scrolls. More people joined in the effort to send out the word of the Esther Fast that evening.

The next morning our Pastoral Care Secretary, Susan Poole, came to me with a list out of the Toronto telephone directory. It contained all the Jewish organizations in the city. Attached to it was a note, "Pastor Williamson, should any of these organizations receive the scroll?" With delight I went ahead and made sure each organization received a copy of the scroll.

By Thursday morning, February 10, the office was buzzing. There were five volunteer secretaries just to handle the contact records of who was receiving copies of the scroll. As I came into my office, the first thing on my mind was to write Dr. Paul Yonggi Cho, pastor of the largest Church in the world in Seoul, Korea. The attendance at his Full Gospel Central Church at that time was between 300,000 and 400,000 people each Sunday. My letter was quite bold:

Dear Dr. Cho,

You gave a word regarding Canada. God in his sovereignty is bringing it to pass in the midst of a forty-fast here at Queensway Cathedral in Toronto, Canada.

I know you are going to call the people of your assembly... to join in this period of special intercession.

So bold I am to say this to you, but it is burning deep in my heart...

Dr. Cho sent an immediate reply dated February 23, 1983 which arrived March 9:

We received your letter of February 10, with a copy of the Word Re The Esther Fast, and we want you to know that the Full Gospel Central Church has joined you in prayer for Israel. We are placing your letter and the fast in our special prayer basket. Over the weekend and during the week thousands of believers will be praying with you in all seven services on Sunday that Israel will be released from her bondage, and that the name of the Lord will be lifted up in Israel! Later a portion of your letter and the Fast will be translated and sent to Prayer Mountain where another group of people who are fasting and praying for hundreds of other needs from around the world will include this request also, with their own. During the week it is possible there may be approximately 3,000 who will be fasting and praying.

Many other things concerning the Esther Fast took place on February 10. Letters similar to the one to Dr. Cho went out to Christian publishers, leaders and pastors. Our volunteer staff began extra mailings. A French copy of the scroll was prepared by a member of our French bible study group. Maggie Larmand, the daughter of Donald Morand, the Ombudsman of Ontario (see chapter 3), began to send letters to the various Ombudsmen around the world. Her letter was discreet and to the point:

I am sure that you are aware that the Jewish people have suffered much under many governments. We as concerned believers wish to draw to your attention a call to a world-wide fast for the Release, Return, and Restoration of the Jewish people. Your assistance in distributing the enclosed Decree will be greatly appreciated.

We have on record nine replies to her letter. Two in particular stand out to me. The first comes from the City Hall in Haifa, Israel:

Dear Maggie,
I wish to confirm receipt of your kind letter of February 10, 1983, and am deeply moved by its contents.

Although I do not claim to be a fervent believer as you and your brethren of faith are, but, as an Ombudsman, an Israeli and a Jew, I feel most encouraged and even cheered by the most noble and commendable act of human solidarity, empathy and brotherly love transpiring from every word and sentence in both your letter and Decree.

I shall consequently willingly pass your message

to interested people and am reiterating my sincere appreciations of your gracious initiative.
Sincerely,

Jacob Levav

The second letter is from C.L. Johnson, the Parliamentary Commissioner for Administrative Investigation (i.e., the ombudsman) in Brisbane, Australia. He reports some of the results of his passing on the news of the Esther Fast:

Dear Mrs. Larmand,
   ...it seems that the Esther Fast was certainly not forgotten as far as Australia is concerned. I say Australia because it seems that it was not only confined to Queensland. For example, one letter I received only last week was in the following terms:

"We have been notifying as many interested people as we can and have roused a good deal of interest. The Baptist Church to which we belong has taken it up seriously besides many of our friends.

There is now a Branch of The International Christian Embassy Jerusalem in Australia. The Director is Mr. John Herzog. He is today in Canberra organising a protest rally to the Soviet Embassy there, for next Saturday. This protest is on an international scale and is part of the "Esther Fast" plan. The protest rally and this Esther Fast are all under the auspices of the ICEJ."

I know also that very positive action was taken by the Salvation Army as well as other denominations.
Yours sincerely,
C.L. Johnson
Commissioner

Coming back to our home base once again, my notes show that on February 11, Gord Holmes of our congregation wrote a splendid letter to then Israeli Prime Minister, Menachem Begin.

Good things were happening at every turn in the road. A German translation of the Esther Fast scroll was prepared by Helmutt Loeffler, one of our ushers, and given to me on Friday, February 18. This was just the beginning of the three days of Holy Convocation which concluded the forty-day fast our church was observing. Within minutes of receiving this translation, a lady approached me requesting copies in the German language. What timing!

Bright and early Monday morning, February 21, with the mighty challenge of the Holy Convocation in my heart, I began three days of sharing about the Esther Fast on "100 Huntley Street." That same afternoon, following the T.V. presentation, Pastor Rutledge and I had a meeting at Holy Blossom Synagogue with several of Toronto's rabbis. We later reported to the Queensway congregation that these Jewish leaders were deeply moved by our sincere desire to see God's Word fulfilled in them as His ancient people.

Every day, when I arrived at the church office, there were more surprises awaiting me. One of these came from Titus Brown in Spanish Town, Jamaica. This brother made it his business to go from church to church giving out the scrolls and sharing the news of the fast.

Then there was Anna. I had never met either Anna, or Doris, the lady who had shared news of the fast with her. It was amazing how friends of friends passed on the word. Anna's letter to me was dated March 10. She reported that she had reprinted the scroll and sent it to both Jewish and Christian people. One of these contacts was so pleased with what he received that he sent out an additional 237 copies of the scroll himself. What amazed and overwhelmed me when I received her final report was that this dear lady had sent out close to 5000 copies of the scroll to many countries around the globe!

On the same day as Anna was sending her report off to me, Judy Carleton of the Queensway congregation happended to be listening to a well-known Toronto radio broadcaster, the late Gordon Sinclair, on a program entitled, "Let's Get Personal." Judy heard Mr. Sinclair making a comment on the then newly-elected Prime Minister of Australia, Robert Hawke. Mr. Hawke had been to Moscow three times to plead for the release of Jewish refuseniks from Russia. The next day, March 11, I took the liberty of writing to the Right Honourable Robert Hawke indicating that I had heard of his trips to Moscow. I voiced my support for his efforts on behalf of Russian Jews and enclosed copies of the scroll which by that date had circulated to fifty different countries. Mr. Hawke's senior advisor replied to this letter expressing Mr. Hawke's appreciation at receiving the materials.

We were excited to learn that in late March, the *Belfast Telegraph* ran a full-sized copy of the scroll in their "Church Notices" section. This is one of the leading daily newspapers in that Northern Ireland city of half a million.

In the midst of T.V. interviews, news items, and letter writing, people began to share with me what God was showing them in prayer as they would intercede for the Jewish people in Russia. One lady Yvonne Hickson, left a note with me following a prayer meeting she had led on Saturday, March 12. She wrote that while in prayer, she had pictured the walls of Jericho as walls of opposition to the release of the Jewish refuseniks from Russia. As she prayed, suddenly, she saw a door in the walls burst open and numbers of Jewish people running toward her. It appeared that they were being pushed from behind. At first Yvonne noticed that their faces looked bewildered and they appeared not to know where they were headed. But, as these people got closer to Yvonne and to those who had formed a prayer line around the walls, the look of bewilderment left their faces.

This particular vision seems to line up with Jeremiah 23:7-8. We are now engaged in a battle of prayer for the release of Soviet Jewish refuseniks. As God's people pray, God is working to see the trickle of release grow. This is going to continue until the great release spoken of by Jeremiah.

The same day Yvonne Hickson saw this vision in prayer, March 12, I found a significant item on page 8 of the *Toronto Globe and Mail*. It was a report concerning Soviet Jews. Here it is word for word:

SOVIET JEWS

The Third International Soviet Jewry Conference will take place in Jerusalem from March 14 to 17. At that time, world Jewry will gather to express its anxiety at the new repressions practiced against Jews in the Soviet Union and will show its solidarity and commitment to this isolated and victimized Jewish "community," the third largest in the world.

Today, the very existence of Soviet Jews is at stake. Not only has emigration from the Soviet Union virtually stopped, but all expressions of Jewish identity have been ruthlessly suppressed. Jewish activists are in prison or in exile. Jewish seminars, whether secular, religious or cultural, have been disrupted; telephone links with the outside world have been severely restricted – all with the expressed aim to achieve the disintegration of the Jewish community.

Those gathered in Jerusalem in March will announce to the world that they care and that they will continue the struggle on behalf of their brothers and sisters in the Soviet Union. They will cry out the Soviet authorities: "Let our people go."

Jeanette Goldman
Chairman,
Committee for Soviet Jewry,
Toronto

This article added fuel to the fires of our intercession for Soviet Jews. *The Toronto Star* on Wednesday, March 16, had an article entitled, "'Let Soviet Jews out' – U.S." It was a report on the Third International Soviet Jewry Conference mentioned in the *Globe and Mail* article quoted above. Although it is old news now, a summary of its contents is worth repeating as to this moment, things have not changed substantially:

JERUSALEM (UPI) – The U.S. ambassador to Israel, Samuel Lewis, has attacked Soviet policies that have cut the emigration of Russian Jews to a "pathetic trickle" and said such abuses impede efforts to improve Moscow-Washington relations.

As Lewis addressed the American delegates to the Third World Conference on Soviet Jewry[sic], there were isolated grumblings that the participants weren't angry enough over the freeze in emigration and abuse of Russian Jews.

"Soviet abuses of human rights and specifically

of the rights of Soviet Jews are a major obstacle to any effort to improve U.S.-Soviet relations," Lewis said, adding the policy has been made clear to Moscow.

He said all U.S. efforts on behalf of Soviet Jews can't be made public but that the feeling of frustration over the Soviets' hard stand is universal in Washington.

"Every American official who has any dealings with this issue from the president down shares the bitter disappointment... with Soviet intransigence on this question... (and) with the sharp decline in the number of Jews permitted to emigrate from the Soviet Union, now down to a pathetic trickle," he said.

Emigration of Jews from the Soviet Union dropped to 2,688 in 1982 from a high of 51,320 in 1979. So far this year (1983) it is 204.

Another 400,000 Soviet Union Jews want to leave, said Joseph Smukler, chairman of the American delegation. "At stake now is the survival of 20 per cent of our people and the fibre and mettle of the remainder," he added.

Is it any wonder after reading the above that I turn to the next key item in my diary of events and find that a dear friend, Bob Gal, called at 11:55 a.m. on March 22 to share Psalm 106:44-48,

44 But he took note of their distress
when he heard their cry;
45 for their sake he remembered his covenant
and out of his great love he relented.
46 He caused them to be pitied
by all who held them captive.
47 Save us, O Lord our God,
and gather us from the nations,
that we may give thanks to your holy name
and glory in your praise.
48 Praise be to the Lord, the God of Israel,
from everlasting to everlasting.
Let all the people say, "Amen!"

I felt the cry of intercession as I read verse 46 that day in March. But, as I read my diary in preparation to write this chapter, I simply burst into tears. God is going to do it friends. He, the God of Abraham, Isaac, and Jacob is going to work the mighty miracle of bringing His people back to their land. That is why we have fasted and prayed and that is why, with God's help, we shall do it again and again for the glory of our Father in heaven – until the answer comes.

CHAPTER FIVE

Release and Return

It was Thursday evening, March 31, 1983. All over the globe those who had chosen to participate in the Esther Fast were preparing to begin their fast the next day. The mandate on the Esther Fast scroll was before them to pray for the Release, Return, Restoration, and Revival of both Israel and the Church of Jesus Christ.

As a final step of preparation for the fast, our church invited a very special guest to speak on two of the key prayer targets: Release and Return. Avigdor Eskin came to us highly recommended by Mario Biaggi and Robert K. Dornan, both members of the United State's Congress and Evangelist Gerald Derstine of Christian Retreat in Florida. A quote from Mr. Dornan's letter of introduction gives some details on Mr. Eskin's background:

Mr. Eskin lived the first 19 of his 21 years in the Soviet Union. As an organizer of classes and teacher of Hebrew and religious studies in Moscow, he faced persecution from the Soviet government. After many arrests the communists decided to let Avigdor emigrate to Israel two years ago (1979) rather than deal with him for the rest of his life. The Soviets unleashed a man of God who is now on a mission to spread the word about the mistreatment of religious groups behind the Iron Curtain.

Avigdor believes in the Bible and strongly feels that people must live the Bible. He is saddended by the moral decay in Western societies, and worries that Americans do not appreciate the freedom we enjoy. I know many people will be interested, as I, in hearing how this young man, who had no faith in God, is now being used by God to fight for the right of the people to study scripture in the language of the Bible.

Having spoken with Avigdor by telephone on a couple of previous occasions, I felt a genuine warmth toward this courageous young man. When we finally did meet that day in the lobby of his Toronto hotel, we immediately embraced and within moments were conversing like old friends. Avigdor was obviously very intelligent. But what touched me most was his love for the Lord, his love of the Scriptures, and his desire to see Soviet Jews free to worship God in their own language. He was fascinated to know why I, as a Christian, had committed myself to the Esther Fast on behalf of Soviet Jews.

When I questioned him on his personal relationship with God, Avigdor responded by relating an experience he had while in prison in Russia. Another Jewish prisoner had been sharing with him some prayers he had received through Dr. Joseph Begun, a well-known refusenik, now in prison.[1] Avigdor started praying these prayers and felt that God answered him for the first time in his life. Up to this time he confessed that he did not know God. Following this experience, however, he started to pray on a regular basis. What interested me most was his statement that God did not always answer his prayers, and yet, in spite of this, he declared with great delight that God is a mighty God who hears the prayers of one in prison. He went on to compare his prison experience to that of Joseph in the Bible. He was awestruck that the God of Joseph would answer his prayers.

That evening the meeting hall at our church was packed to capacity with over 500 people. In his address, Avigdor expanded on our conversation of that afternoon. His remarks are best summarized in a paper he left with me entitled, "Soviet Jewry – What Christians Can Do." Here is an edited version of the paper:

SOVIET JEWRY –
WHAT CHRISTIANS CAN DO

It was more than 2000 years ago when the Jewish prophet Ezekiel saw a valley full of dry bones and God asked him the crucial question: "Can these bones live?" The answer was given by the Lord Himself for all the coming generations: "These bones are the whole House of Israel, behold, they say, 'our bones are dried and our hope is lost: we are clean cut off.' Therefore, prophesy and say to them, 'thus says the Lord God: behold, my people, I will open your graves and bring you into the land of Israel.'"

We are a witness to the fulfillment of that prophecy in Communist Russia today. The people who denied God came to power in October 1917 and a part of their terrible terror was from the very beginning an attempt to destroy spiritually the Jewish community....

The Jewish minority in Russia was always persecuted. Thousands of them were sacrificed in pogroms in the times of the Czars. At the beginning of the 1900s, the Zionist organization of Russia was estimated at 300,000 active members. When there were elections to a Jewish assembly in 1918, the Zionists got over 60% and the communists

63

only 5%. Thus, the communists did not represent the Jewish community at all, but it was even worse. Together with their Party friends, they participated in such wild terror against religious and Zionist Jews that all the persecutions of the Czars seemed small in comparison.

Synagogues were closed and destroyed, rabbis were sent to Siberia. Hebrew, the language of the Holy Bible, was proclaimed as "alien and reactionary." No book has been published in Hebrew in the USSR since 1927. The gates of Russia closed and only a few were lucky enough to leave. All Jewish schools were shut, and all legal ways to study Judaism and Jewish culture were ended.... No Zionist or any other Jewish organization was left after 1926, but it was only a prelude to the horror of Stalin.

Stalin's terror, which caused tens of millions to perish, was especially hard on Jews. All Jewish schools were closed and Jewish culture, even in Yiddish, was prohibited. Jewish actors and poets were murdered, and every Jewish family lost members. Emigration to Israel became almost impossible since 1926, and only after international pressure was brought to bear were some Jews able to leave....

Stalin planned his final solution to the Jewish question after the infamous "Jewish doctors' plot." Special railroads were built to Siberia, and it was planned that by the end of 1953 Russia would be *judenrein* (free of Jews). But God was kind to His people and Stalin died on March 5, 1953. How many Jews were killed during those terrible times? Some researchers say half a million, some say a million and a half, but who knows the real truth?

After Stalin's death came what was called liberalization. Many people were released from concentration camps, but Jewish culture still remained prohibited and the doors of Russia were still closed.

And the free world completely forgot about Soviet Jews. When Golda Meir arrived in Moscow in 1948 as the first Israeli ambassador, she was greeted by a massive throng of Jews near the Moscow synagogue. "Praise God that we could live so long to see such a glorious day," she whispered. Many of those who dared to express their desire to return to the Holy Land paid with their freedom.

Even after the worst days of terror there were Jews who lived only for a dream – to come back to Zion. In Riga, Kiev, and Moscow, visiting Israeli artists and sports teams were greeted by cheering crowds of Soviet Jews, who found a way to express themselves. And this was only the tip of the iceberg of the Zionist underground network in Russia. Thousands of books and Hebrew self-teaching materials were distributed unofficially every year by Jewish activists. The tension continued to grow, and in 1970 the whole world heard for the first time of the plight of Soviet Jews: a group of young Jews attempted to steal a Soviet airplane and escape to Israel. After their arrest a huge public protest took place in the West. This was the beginning of the struggle for Soviet Jewry. Over 260,000 have been allowed to leave, but how many remain? We cannot rely on official Soviet statistics; estimates vary from three to six million.

After the wave of emigration, the authorities have now virtually stopped Jews from leaving for Israel. Many families were broken up when the Soviets did not allow some members to leave. In terms of emigration, 1981 was the worst year in a decade.

And Jewish culture is still suppressed. I remember one of my first visits to the Moscow Synagogue on Archipova Street when I was 13. There were groups of young Jews who found the only possibility to express their Judaism through singing and dancing on Jewish holidays. The police tried to destroy them, as usual, but the youngsters filled all the space near the synagogue, and were afraid of no one. I was the only one who could sing "Hatikvah", the Israeli national anthem, in Hebrew, and so my voice dominated that evening. It was God who gave us courage to sing the words of Hatikvah right in front of Soviet policemen: "Our hope is still not lost!"

I paid no attention to the policemen who spoke to some strange young men. When I went to the bus, I suddenly saw those young men near me, and they showed me in jest what they were going to do to me. I was stunned. Only then did I realize that these were special KGB brigades who were used for beating and killing, and doing all their dirty work....

They followed me onto the bus, three by the door and five near me. They indicated again and again what they had in store for me, all the while enjoying my horror. My entire life passed before me in short pictures, and I was still naive enough to ask why. But sometimes the Almighty sends His salvation at the best moment. In a state of shock, I turned to a soldier and said, "I was just passing through Archipova Street, and these people have been following me since. Please help me!" He asked me to go with him, and when we got off the bus, eight people went with us, but after a brief conversation amongst themselves, they turned around and went away. That soldier will never know what he did for me.

Many of my friends met the same persecution, but remained strong enough to continue....

Today, many Christians feel that they did not do enough to prevent the Holocaust and they see the Soviet Jewry issue as a means to repent with action and improve the image of Christian morality after the Nazis challenged all the principles of Christianity. The active Christian involvement on behalf of Soviet Jews can relieve the suffering of many people, but it is also important for Christians themselves to participate in fulfilling the words of the prophets and to open a completely new page in Christian-Jewish relations.

Here are some ways individuals and groups can help:

1. Write to a Soviet Jew, encourage him to leave for Israel, give him information about the Holy Land. Send your letter by registered mail with return airmail receipt. If you do not get back the receipt within two months, file a "tracer" at the post office in which you can claim compensation.

2. Send Hebrew teaching books or pictures of Israel to a Soviet Jew. Please do not send missionary material. It will deeply offend the recipient.

3. Send a parcel of new clothing which can be resold privately to support families dismissed from work for applying to emigrate. By Soviet regulation, the clothes must be new.

4. Phone one of the activists via a "messenger call," and let him know about your support.

5. Write to your regional and national government representatives to intervene with Soviet authorities on behalf of a Jew refused permission to leave for Israel (called "refuseniks"), or who was harassed for organizing Jewish studies. Urge him to promote Jewish emigration from Russia and the legalization of unofficial classes of Jewish studies. Ask these representatives to write, call or send Hebrew material to some activists.

6. Try to form a special committee in your church or Christian organization on behalf of Soviet Jewry.

7. Recite special prayers for these suffering people.

8. Call directly to the nearest Soviet embassy or consulate and protest.

9. Take a trip to the USSR and bring Jewish materials and meet with these courageous people.

10. Organize a rally in your community at the nearest Soviet embassy or consulate protesting the restrictions on emigration, and the cultural genocide and imprisonment of Soviet Jews.

In Canada, write to the Committee For Soviet Jewry, Canadian Jewish Congress, 4600 Bathurst Street, Willowdale, Ontario, M2R 3V2. See the Appendices for information regarding other organizations that assist Soviet Jews.

A final thought. Indifference and silence are unacceptable when we deal with saving human beings and fulfilling God's prophecy. Let us hear the cry of the Biblical Mordechai: "If you keep silent at this time, deliverance will come for the Jews from another quarter, but you and your family will be destroyed" (Esther 4:14).

An excellent firsthand account of how one Christian family became involved with the Soviet Jewish refuseniks is found in the book, *Gates of Brass* by Jay and Meridel Rawlings. Jay and Meridel were introduced at the close of chapter 3. Their book provides details on how to become involved in helping Soviet Jews. There is also a film version of *Gates of Brass* distributed by International Vistas, P.O. Box 8232, Jerusalem, Israel 91081. It was during the first Esther Fast, April 1,2, and 3, 1983 that the Rawlings and their twelve-year-old son, Chris were visiting refuseniks in their homes in the Soviet Union. They were representing thousands of Christians who had joined in the worldwide Esther Fast. They themselves had completed the fast at an earlier date due to the strenuous nature of their trip.

Some may ask, How does one go about a three-day fast with no food or drink? I learned how to undertake such a fast over a period of time. During the years 1971 to 1975, I had progressed from fasting one meal to observing a twenty-one-day fast similar to that of Daniel, chapter 10. At that time, I had one glass of warm water and one slice of whole-wheat bread at each mealtime. My own understanding of the subject of fasting has grown significantly through studying a book entitled, *God's Chosen Fast* by Arthur Wallis. This book is one of the best I have found on the topic of fasting. It approaches the subject in a sane and balanced way.

The first record I have of participating in an Esther-type fast is recorded in my diary for January, 1975. A new challenge lay before me in my ministry and I was concerned that I make myself available to the Lord in obedience to His will for my life. In the fall of 1975 I had set out on an itinerary to speak in churches in the Maritime provinces of Canada concerning my mission to French Canada. The thought of fasting was in my mind. When would the Lord give me the go ahead?

Suddenly it happened! Two of the churches I was to hold meetings in cancelled at the very last moment. That left a Monday, Tuesday, and Wednesday with no commitments. I knew that this was the time for my three-day fast. On that day I happened to be in Halifax, Nova Scotia. Ralph Rutledge, whom I had known since Bible College days, was the pastor of the church I was visiting when I received the meeting cancellations. I asked Pastor Rutledge if I could stay with him and his family during the three days of my fast. He graciously obliged. With great joy I completed my fast in the strength of the Lord.

The Lord knows best how to prepare us for the work of His Kingdom. He has the plans laid out for us, and as we walk with Him daily, He is faithful to unfold them one step at a time. He always goes ahead of us to prepare the way well in advance. Thus when it came time for the word on the Esther Fast (January, 1983) which I was now observing with thousands of believers around the world, there was a deep sense of assurance that God was at work in a mighty way to accomplish His purposes. See the Appendices for instructions regarding how to have a three-day Esther Fast.

Thursday, March 31, we had listened closely as Avigdor Eskin shared the plight of Soviet Jewry. The Esther Fast had already begun at 6 p.m. that evening. On Saturday evening, the second day of the fast, we had organized home prayer meetings around the city of Toronto as well as one in our church. The principle of two or three gathering together in agreement according to Matthew 18:19 was powerfully observed as sixteen groups joined in intercession. Each group leader took the, "Prayer for Oppressed Jews" that had been given to us by the Canadian Jewish Congress. It is usually said during the Seder supper at Passover, hence the references to raising cups of wine. It is a prayer for us all to pray until total release of the Jews in all the countries of the world where they suffer at this moment.

PRAYER FOR OPPRESSED JEWS
(Read by the leader or said responsively):

As God commands us to remember the sufferings of all people, even our enemies, let us remember the Jews who suffer today under oppression and persecution, let us lessen our rejoicing as we think of their plight, and let us vow to help.

We were Pharoah's slaves in Egypt –
And Moses led us to freedom,
We were a people with no homeland –
To Eretz (the land of) Israel you brought us.
In thanks we praise Thee, O Lord,
In joy we drink the wine.

We were enslaved again in Europe
And the hand of Death descended,
We wandered without shelter

'Til again you brought us home.
    In mourning we extoll Thee, O Lord,
    In remembrance we pour the wine.

Some of us still live in darkness –
With fear and death ever present,
We pray for a new exodus
To deliver our people from bondage.
    In despair we beseech Thee, O Lord,
    In sorrow we raise the wine.

(Raise cups):

Our cups raised, for tens of thousands
Held captive, persecuted, threatened,
Our cups raised – a prayer for deliverance,
Our cups raised – our promise to help.
    With hope we pray to Thee, O Lord,
    To action we dedicate ourselves.

O Lord our God, who rescued us from Egypt,
who returned us to Jerusalem,
help us to save our brothers, your children,
wherever they are in danger.

(All participants say in unison):
    With each community that suffers
    Our cup of joy is lessened:
        Ethiopia
        Iran
        Russia
        Syria
    May we all soon be safe.
    Amen.

(Lower cups)

Following the prayer for oppressed Jews along with many other requests for both Israel and the Church, the prayer groups were invited to review some of the Scriptures listed below related to the return of the Jewish people to their land.

Genesis – 12:1-4.
Numbers – 34:1-12.
Deuteronomy – 8:6-10; 11:8-9; 30:1-6.
Psalms – 126:1-6; 147:1-6.
Isaiah – 11:11-12; 14:1; 27:12-13; 35:1-10; 40:1-2, 9-11; 49:13-23; 51:3, 11-13; 61:3-9; 62:1-12; 66:7-14.
Jeremiah – 30:3-11, 17-24; 31:1-14; 32:40-44; 33:9-11.
Ezekiel – 11:16-20; 28:25-26; 34:11-16; 36:1-38; 37:1-14; 38:1-23; 39:21-29.
Joel – 2:18-19, 21-27.
Amos – 9:14-15.
Micah – 2:12.
Zephaniah – 3:14-20.
Zechariah – 2:1-13; 8:1-23; 10:6-10.

The following Scriptures refer specifically to the Exodus of the Jews from Russia:

Isaiah – 43:5-6.
Jeremiah – 3:11-18; 16:14-15; 23:1-8; 31:1-14.
Zechariah – 2:6-9.

An excellent book to read on this second Exodus is *EXODUS II, Let My People Go!* by Steve Lightle. It relates the amazing story of how God has been speaking independently to many individuals in Finland, Sweden, and other parts of Europe asking them to prepare to receive a great exodus of Jewish people as they flee from Russia. It provides firm documentation that it is indeed the Lord who has been speaking to His people on an individual basis without them consulting with each other in preparation for this great release from the north that is the focus of the prayers of the Esther Fast.

On Sunday morning, April 3, Pastor Jim Cantelon spoke in our two Sunday morning services on the topic, "Pray for the peace of Jerusalem" (Psalm 122:6). Rani Gauthier, the wife of the elder, Jacques Gauthier, referred to in chapter 2, wrote a poem entitled, "Israel." We were so deeply touched with it that the Pastor gave permission for it to appear in the church bulletin that week. It provides a fitting conclusion to this chapter.

ISRAEL

Israel, Israel,
The apple of my eye,
Do you not know
The measure of my love for you?
Do you not know
That I parted the seas for you?
Do you not know
That I provided for you
In the wilderness?
Do you not know
Of my promises
To your descendents of old?
Do you not know
That the light of the world
Has been appointed
To shine through you?
   Turn to me now, Israel
   For I again
   Turn my face to you
   And call you
   To be my friend
   So that again,
   I may speak to you
   Of mysteries divine;

The time has come
For me to again
Encircle you with my arms
And cover you with my loving-kindness
The hour has come
For all to see
The glory of the God of Israel!

Rani Gauthier

Footnote

1. *While the proofs were being read for this book, the joyous*
   news of Dr. Begun's release was received in the West
   in late February.

CHAPTER SIX

The Vanguard of Praise

Anatoly Shcharansky's picture sat in front of me on my desk. I began to read the accompanying article from the International Christian Embassy in Jerusalem: "Soviet Jewish Prisoner of Conscience. Born: 20 January 1948; Family: Avital; Profession: Mathematician; Date of Arrest: 15 March, 1977; Dates of Trial: 15 March, 1977 and 10-14 July, 1978; Charge: "Treason"; Sentence: 13 years, 3 in prison, 10 in labour camps; Prison address: U.S.S.R. Moscow UCHR 5110/1 UE."

Now we can look back at the splendid news of his release from prison and subsequent reunion with his wife, Avital in Israel in February of 1986. But, at that time, in 1983, the news was far from good. His hunger strike of 1982 was history, but many of his family, friends, and fellow Jews were greatly concerned for his health. They were doing all they could to help by putting pressure on the Soviet government. There were also many people praying for Mr. Shcharansky.

At the same time I was reading the article from the International Christian Embassy, I received an encouraging note concerning Mr. Shcharansky from Gladys Yasinski, a member of the Canadian Friends of the International Christian Embassy. She wrote:

> Anatoly Shcharansky has spent time in solitary confinement in a Russian prison memorizing the Psalms. His eyes are too bad to read the small book of Psalms so he has copied them out and committed them to memory.

For more information on this courageous refusenik, read Martin Gilbert's book entitled, *Shcharansky: Hero of Our Time*. David Kilgour, a Canadian Member of Parliament, calls it a "superb biography." This same Martin Gilbert is featured in the International Vistas Film entitled, *Gates of Brass*.

Knowing of my keen interest in Russian Jews, people from our congregation began to hand me newspaper clippings, letters, and even telephone to convey the news they had heard over the radio or seen on television. This included information about Christian as well as Jewish prisoners of conscience in the Soviet Union.

Step by step I was getting answers to some key questions I had been asking myself for a good while. Did I really appreciate my freedom of speech and my freedom of religion? Was I really taking advantage of my freedom to help others who needed me to pray for them and to speak out on their behalf? Was I going to allow all the legitimate needs of my own life to crowd out the needs of the rest of the world?

Prior to the Esther Fast itself, plans were already underway to launch a Jehoshaphat March of Victory and Praise. The impetus for this project came from a sermon Pastor Ralph Rutledge had preached at the beginning of 1983. His message, taken from 2 Chronicles 20:1-30, was entitled, "The Vanguard of Praise." He placed particular emphasis on verses 15b and 20-22:

This is what the Lord says to you: "Do not be afraid or discouraged because of this vast army. For the battle is not yours, but God's...."

Early in the morning they left for the Desert of Tekoa. As they set out, Jehoshaphat stood and said, "Listen to me, Judah and people of Jerusalem! Have faith in the Lord your God and you will be upheld; have faith in his prophets and you will be successful." After consulting the people, Jehoshaphat appointed men to sing to the Lord and to praise him for the splendor of his holiness as they went out ahead of the army, saying:

"Give thanks to the Lord,
 for his love endures forever."

As they began to sing and praise, the Lord set ambushes against the men of Ammon and Moab and Mount Seir who were invading Judah, and they were defeated.

When the Lord God of the universe speaks and we obey Him, miraculous things are bound to happen. A number of people began to sense that God was calling us to hold a victory march similar to that of King Jehoshaphat. It was a call not only to humble ourselves, but also to praise the Lord for victory in relation to the future fulfillment of God's word in Jeremiah 16:14-15 and 23:7-8. In Jeremiah 31:7 we read,

This is what the Lord says:
"Sing with joy for Jacob;
 shout for the greatest of the nations.
Make your praises heard, and say,
 'O Lord, save your people,
 the remnant of Israel.'"

(Emphasis mine. See Revelation 7:4-8 which also refers to this "remnant of Israel.")

Verse 8 goes on to tell about the release not only from the north, but from the ends of the earth. Further insight comes as we read verse 10:

Hear the word of the Lord, O nations; *proclaim it in distant coastlands*:

"He who scattered Israel will gather them
and will watch over His flock like a Shepherd."

(Emphasis mine.)

The message does not end here. Open your Bible and read verses 11-14. The battle still rages, but the victory is sure. I was convinced this march should be our public proclamation of the victory for which we had sought God in the Esther Fast. Our praises must be heard!

Having set matters in motion for the march prior to the Esther Fast, I had communicated the need for a co-ordinated effort to Valentyna Polakiwsky, one of the volunteer secretaries of our assembly. Valentyna agreed to be the march co-ordinator. Thanks to her efficiency, in a matter of a few days we were sending out invitations to participate in the march to all the appropriate laymen, pastors, churches, and organizations.

We invited Dr. David Lewis, President of Christians United for Israel, to be the guest speaker at the public rally following the march. He had held a week of meetings at Queensway Cathedral immediately following the Esther Fast. His prophetic teaching on Israel was dynamic. Dr. Lewis' next engagement after leaving our church was in Ottawa, our nation's capital. Dr. Lewis, Alan Lazerte, Executive Director of Canadian Friends of the International Christian Embassy, and I planned to meet in Ottawa on Monday, April 18. We had all been invited to attend a special open house at the residence of the

Israeli Ambassador. The purpose was to celebrate the thirty-fifth anniversary of Israel's independence. What happened on the way to Ottawa was an unusual example of God's perfect timing.

As I boarded Air Canada Flight 444 early on the morning of April 18, I spotted the Honourable David Smith, a Member of Parliament. I had met David through his brother, Pastor Bob Smith who had been my classmate in Bible College. I had spoken with David briefly on several occasions at various public functions. Today, however, it was different. His greeting seemed more friendly than usual. There was no opportunity to talk as the aisle of the plane was filled with businessmen looking for their seats so I returned his greeting and took my seat. David continued down the aisle.

During the fifty-minute flight, I began to ask the Lord why I was on the same flight as David Smith on such a special day. It did not take long for the answer to come. When we arrived in Ottawa, I was ahead of David walking into the terminal. I walked slowly to let him catch up. Once again we shared hellos. David asked me how things were going and the reason for my visit to Ottawa.

"Fine," I replied. "I'm here today to celebrate the thirty-fifth anniversary of Israel's independence."

"Well, that's interesting," said David, "I'll be there myself!"

Then I asked him about his association with the Israeli Ambassador. He said he had recently returned from his fourth trip to the Soviet Union.

"I'm Chairman of the Canadian Parliamentary Group for Soviet Jewry."

I could not believe my ears. I wanted to shout, "Hallelujah!" I spent the next few moments relating to David the initial results of the Esther Fast and telling him about the upcoming Jehoshaphat Victory March. One thing led to another until I was writing down an appointment with David Smith at the Parliament Buildings for 5 p.m. I mentioned that I was with Dr. David Lewis and Alan Lazerte and asked if he would mind if they joined me. David was delighted.

The celebration of the thirty-fifth anniversary of Israel's independence that afternoon was held at the residence of the Israeli Ambassador, Yeshayahu Anug. Dr. Lewis, Alan Lazerte and I were introduced as a group to Mr. Anug by Evangelist Bill Prankard who was well known to the embassy for his very strong support for the State of Israel. Mr. Prankard also introduced us to several others including Mr. Uriel Savir, the embassy's Second Secretary. I hardly knew what to do with myself when the introductions were complete except enjoy some of the delicious hors d'oeuvres that were being served. Catching a whisper of conversation here and there, I concluded that everyone in the room was trying to come up with solutions to Israel's problems. I had several enjoyable conversations that afternoon with the various guests.

Our 5 p.m. appointment with David Smith was a memorable one. What was to have been a brief appointment lasted over an hour as David gave us a summary of the Canadian position on the refusenik question. David Smith was clear and to the point about the violations of the Helsinki Accord of August 1, 1975. He stated that the Soviet Union was clearly using its unjust treatment of various ethnic groups as a bargaining tool in international negotiations.

The things I learned that day have been further supported by information I receive regularly from the then new Chairman of the Soviet Jewry Committee, Mr. David Kilgour, Member of Parliament for Edmonton-Strathcona. Mr. Kilgour, speaking at the annual meeting of the International Commission of Jurists (Canadian Section) on August 20, 1986, began his address as follows:

> It is an honour to speak to you in a personal capacity today on the intractable subject of East-West relations and the international rule of law. The particular focus will be on the many-venued Conference on Security and Cooperation in Europe, its recent and upcoming meetings, and the current utility of the CSCE process.
>
> My argument, a paradoxical one, is that those in the West and neutral countries concerned about improving East-West relations should devote more time and effort in attempting to persuade the government of the Soviet Union to improve basic human rights throughout the Soviet Bloc....
>
> One Soviet argument heard at CSCE meetings is that the restoration of detente would lead to greater respect for human rights by the Soviet government, while international tension would lead to a clamp-down.... Ambassador Richard Schifter of the U.S. delegation at the Human Rights Experts meeting in Ottawa last year dealt with that proposition as follows:
>
> "Does it stand to reason that if foreign countries establish friendly relations with a particular government that government in turn will – so to speak – reward the foreign countries by dealing kindly with its own citizens? And does it further stand to reason that if international relations are tense, the foreign countries will be punished by the government in question through the adoption of rep-

ressive measures against its own citizens? Would this not mean that a government holds its own people hostage, treating them well or poorly depending on the way other countries treat it in international affairs?"

Our visit with David Smith concluded with a tour of the main floor of the Central Block of the Parliament Buildings and a visit to the House of Commons itself. Following this unusual day in Ottawa, the Holy Spirit reminded me of the words that I had spoken on Tuesday evening, February 1, 1983 at Queensway Cathedral, "God is going to open doors into governments... for the Esther Fast."

To return to the Jehoshaphat Victory March, regrettably, Dr. Lewis was not able to be the guest speaker at the march due to illness. The events of the march were admirably reported by Valentyna Polakiwsky in Dr. Lewis' paper, *Jerusalem Courier and Prophecy Digest*, Succoth, 1983. Here is a portion of her article:

A Victory March is called! We *will* march in praise, song and thanksgiving to God for the release and return of His ancient people Israel from the North (Soviet Union) (Jeremiah 16:15) and their return from all corners of the earth (Ezekiel 36:24,26) to "their land that I gave unto their fathers."

The date for the *Jehoshaphat Victory March* was confirmed by the Lord to be Sunday, May 22, 1983. We could almost hear the Lord saying to us as He spoke to Jehoshaphat and his people, "Thus said the Lord unto you, *Be not afraid* nor dismayed by reason of this great multitude; for *the battle is not yours, but God's...*

Whilst in prayer for the preparation of this glorious event, the Lord revealed that He would also have us pray and march for the release from the prison camps of the Communist for the *Ukrainians, Poles, Bulgarians, Latvians, Hungarians, Estonians,*

Russians, Lithuanians, Romanians, East Germans and Czechs, of which there are countless thousands upon thousands.

The response from the Jewish people contacted was disbelief and joy....

Upon contacting Sam Resnick of the Canadian Jewish Congress with this proclamation for the Victory March – he quietly ...slowly asked, "Run that date by me again...! Why that's the day that the Jews will be holding their solidarity march in New York! We're expecting over 150,000 Jews to participate," he burst out, "WOW!" Praise the Lord, another confirmation.

Interest calls began to pour into the office as both Jews and Christians consented to participate.

The program was laid out and put together by the Holy Spirit. Pastor Clyde Williamson was the speaker; Dr. Kenneth Robinson, Member of Parliament, made a special trip from our capital, Ottawa, to bring greeting.

The march permit and police escort secured, about one thousand of us gathered in the pouring rain at Nathan Phillips Square [in front of Toronto's City Hall]. When the appointed time arrived to form the groups for marching, the downpour stopped, just at the precise moment. Oh, His faithfulness.

Joyfully leading the march, Ija Artyokow and Gwen Rodkin, two of our faithful intercessors and prayer warriors, unfurled the twenty-foot banner that read boldly *Jehoshaphat Victory March*. Behind them, hearts beating with anticipation, Gladys Yasinski and Barbara Bedford were firmly and proudly displaying the banner with the verse from Joel 2:21 – *"Fear not, O land; be glad and rejoice: for the LORD will do great things,"* in Hebrew. Behind them, Valentyn and Valentyna Polakiwsky carried their banner inscribed in Ukrainian..." *This is My commandment, that ye love one another...,"* (John 15:12).

The next row, the speakers and the representatives of each nation holding high their individual flags, were followed by the rest of the throng....

At the Legislative Building at Queen's Park, everything was set up and waiting for the Word to come forth. Don Brown and Ralph Paddle led the crowd in selected praise choruses. Dr. Robinson brought his greeting. Gail Moore sang out in full voice "Hiney Ma Tov" from Psalm 133, followed by the beautiful, melodic Ukrainian song of "Thanksgiving" by Valentyn and Valentyna [Polakiwsky].

Pastor Williamson stepped forth and the Lord spoke through him with authority and conviction – Yes, Lord, all nations *shall* be greatly affected by whatever transpires in Your nation, Israel.

As Pastor Williamson led us in song with "How Great Thou Art," we concluded our march and greeted one another with hugs and handshakes, all visibly touched by the event....

We had held the Esther Fast. We had celebrated the Jehoshaphat Victory March. What was to come next? Had this call been a one-time event? Was this all the Lord wanted us to do on behalf of His people? Or was there to be a more definite link with His chosen nation and their ancient land?

CHAPTER SEVEN

Kerith is Born

The pull to Israel was getting stronger with each passing day. What did the Lord have in store? In seeking an answer to this question, I made up my mind I would just keep searching the Word, praying, and listening to His voice in the daily events of my life. I knew my Heavenly Father was looking for a yielded vessel through whom He could work.

Following our first trip to Israel in the summer of 1980, I had begun to pray for a Jewish counterpart in Israel who was willing to work with a Canadian Christian in building a bridge of love and trust between Canada and Israel as well as between Jewish and Christian people. There had to be a connecting link. I prayed this way faithfully until the beginning of 1984. I simply kept asking the Father to make the choice and bring that person across my path.

On the afternoon of Sunday, January 15, 1984, my wife, Marion, and I had a most unusual time of prayer. There was a strong sense of expectation. God was about to answer our prayer. We sensed somehow that we were entering a new phase regarding this link with Israel.

Not quite a month later a telephone message was left at the church office in my absence from a Colonel Yehuda Levy. I was to call him at the Sheraton Centre Hotel in downtown Toronto. At first I could not understand why an Israeli Colonel would want to get in touch with me. I called the hotel and asked for Colonel Yehuda Levy. Upon finding out the purpose of his call, my heart leapt with joy in anticipation of what was about to transpire. Colonel Levy and I made plans to get together immediately.

We both had a genuine sense of friendship from the first handshake in the lobby of his hotel. As we sat over lunch that day, he described how he had seen my name on a business card in the Toronto offices of El Al, the Israeli national airline. The card had been left there because I was the National Chairman of the Canadian Friends of the International Christian Embassy in Jerusalem. For some reason, after seeing my name on that card, he found himself wanting to rush back to his hotel and give me a call. This he had done immediately and here we were.

As our conversation continued, Colonel Levy related how he and his family had come from Israel to live in Vancouver on Canada's west coast from 1978 to 1981. He was serving as the Israeli Emissary for the Jewish National Fund for the Province of British Columbia. It was while in this position that he and his wife had had a most unusual experience in one of Vancouver's leading churches. He was invited to come and address the congregation. Being somewhat apprehensive as a Jew about accepting an invitation to speak at a Christian church, he asked his wife, Nitza, to come along and provide moral support. To their utter amazement and delight, he and Nitza were given a very warm reception.

The church choir and congregation filled the sanctuary with Hebrew-style Christian music. The entire service was somewhat overwhelming. The pastor and congregation showed true unconditional love to Colonel Levy and his wife. They were accepted without intimidation or confrontation. How could this be? Could there be such a church that was willing to accept a Jew as a Jew with no strings attached? Never in his life had he believed that such a thing was possible. The deepest desire of that congregation was to build a relationship of love and trust with Jewish people.

As I sat there listening I was enthralled. Here was an Israeli Colonel, born in Jaffa (Jonah's City), a Sabra (born in Israel) whose family had lived in Israel for at least thirteen generations, from a family named, "Levy" (descendants of the tribe of Levi). It is even possible that his family had lived in Israel since biblical times. I felt like I was talking to a walking history book.

Colonel Levy said that upon his return to Israel in 1981, he had to make a choice about his future. He was about to retire from regular service in the Israeli Defense Forces and join the reserves. This meant he had to find a civilian job. One opportunity open to him involved representing the government of Isreal to the churches of North America. This had been under discussion because of the unusual opportunities that had come his way to speak in many churches while he was in Vancouver. Another option was to enter a partnership in a travel company. As Colonel Levy reflected on his options, the choice became clear. He would choose the travel business. He believed this was the best way to build better relations between Jewish and Christian people, and between Israel and the rest of the world. The travel business would allow him to form many personal relationships with individual Christians rather than more formal relationships with church representatives. That luncheon conversation came to a conclusion with the hopes and dreams of four years suddenly beginning to crystallize. Colonel Levy would begin to make preparations for a very special tour to Israel.

It was later on that I discovered Colonel Levy had been involved in some very key events since he left Canada in 1981. His first active duty in the reserves of the Israeli Defense Forces was that of military spokesman in Beirut for several months during the last war in Lebanon. During and after that war he was sent on speaking tours to North America where he appeared on dozens of television and radio shows. He also spoke in many churches and synagogues. In late July of 1982, he had the honour of speaking before a group of congressmen and senators on Capitol Hill in Washington.

Colonel Levy called me at 5 p.m. on February 15 from Edmonton, Alberta to indicate that he had been working on an itinerary which would provide a trip to Israel with a difference. We concluded that for first-time visitors, seeing the historic Christian and Jewish sights was a must. But we also agreed that they should be brought face to face with the people and places of modern Israel. We wanted those on tour to come to grips with Israel both in the past and the present. The present must include identifying with Israel in both her joys and her sorrows. We wanted our guests to return home and tell their friends what Israel is really about today, and then invite them to return with them the next year.

Things were now beginning to come into focus. Specific plans were coming together for me to work with this man whose vision was to build a bridge of love between Christians and Israel. Could this be the Israeli I had been praying for since 1980? As I pondered this question, it occurred to me that a Canadian organization had to be formed to act as a counterpart for Colonel Levy's *Bridge of Love* organization. Up to this point, it had simply been a matter for prayer.

In reflecting on this I began to reveiw my diary. What stood out was an experience I had while in Quebec City on July 11, 1981 as I read 1 Kings 17:3, "Leave here, turn eastward and hide in the Kerith Ravine, east of the Jordan." The key at that time was the word, "Kerith." I wanted to know what this word meant so I looked it up in my concordance. Kerith was a brook in the ancient land of Israel. The meaning given was, "a cut." What an appropriate name for a brook, I thought. A brook cuts its way through the land. The concordance indicated that this word, "kerith" came from a root word, "karath." This root word is a verb and means, "to cut, to cut off, to cut down, or cut asunder" which by implication means to destroy or consume. Now this act of cutting specifically meant, "to covenant" that is, to make an alliance or bargain, originally by cutting up sacrificial animals and passing between the pieces (Genesis 15:9-10, 17-21). This root word is also used in 2 Chronicles 7:18 which says that God, "covenanted" with David to establish his throne forever over Israel.

What then fascinated me as I continued to read my diary was a message from another pastor friend, Don Krohn, who prayed for me two days later. In his prayer he said, "I see you, Clyde, in a desert with a stream coming out of your mouth. You are planting flowers in the desert and it is beginning to bloom." This certainly sounded like Israel to me. When I read this in my diary, I knew instantly that this Canadian counterpart organization was about to be born. Was it to be Kerith Travel? Kerith Shalom? Or what?

I decided to take a step of faith with my lawyer and have a name search done with the provincial government. We found that "Kerith" was available to be used as the name for a registered company. What I was to do with it at that moment, I was not quite sure, but we went ahead and registered the name. I knew my Heavenly Father was leading me.

A letter from Colonel Levy arrived by special delivery in late February. It contained a personal note plus five pages of details concerning a trip itinerary for Israel. I could hardly believe that plans were already underway for our first tour to Israel.

What really surprised me was when I received a call at 11 a.m., Wednesday, March 14 from Colonel Levy. He said he was in the process of getting me a ticket to fly to Israel so that I could have a firsthand view of things. He and I would discuss future tours and lay plans for the *Bridge of Love* program. I would also be able to meet his family and we would all celebrate Passover together.

During the days that followed, I had a very

strong desire to read the Book of Ezra. Two friends, neither one of whom knew the other, and neither one of whom knew that I had been reading the Book of Ezra, spoke to me within two or three hours of one another on Saturday, March 17, 1984. They said that they believed the Lord wanted me to read the Book of Ezra. Needless to say, I read Ezra with great fervency. To my amazement only one verse stood out to me in the entire book. It was Ezra 8:31, "On the twelfth of the first month we set out... to go to Jerusalem." Was I to be in Jerusalem on the twelfth day of April? Well if this was the Lord, then He would work it out. I shared this verse with Pastor Rutledge and asked him to present my trip to Israel to our church board. The following Thursday, Pastor Rutledge indicated that I should move ahead with my plans regarding Israel with great caution.

One day later, Colonel Levy called again from Israel indicating that he had been in touch with El Al Airlines and that I should call a Mr. Telem at my earliest convenience. That afternoon I visiting Mr. Telem's office only to learn that no seats were available on flights for the week of April 12. Nothing else in the immediate future but this week was available on my church calendar, thus, the only week I was free, there were no flights available. What should I do?

I told Mr. Telem I would get back to him as soon as I could work out a suitable date. That evening as I prayed, I felt good about calling Mr. Telem back and asking him to put my name down as a standby for the flight on April 9. This I did the next day. He was most gracious in assuring me that the flight was completely booked, but he would follow my instructions. When I told Pastor Rutledge about the flight situation, I was delightfully surprised at his reply: "If you get that flight, Clyde," he said, with a sparkle in his eyes, "then I'll know this is really the Lord."

The fifth of April was a most unusual day. After leading staff devotions, I returned to my office where I bumped into Pastor Bob Gal. He had come to see Pastor Rutledge and me to show us a beautiful set of slides illustrating the Tabernacle. This was very significant since the Holy Spirit had been prompting me to study the Tabernacle for the last year. I knew it was time to begin that study in earnest. What was even more significant came later in my office. I had asked Bob to pray for me regarding the trip to Israel. While he prayed, I felt the Lord tell me to open my Bible. I flipped it open and looked down. My eyes fell on two words in Isaiah 30:8, "Now go." Was this the confirmation I was seeking? I picked up the telephone to call Mr. Telem one last time to see if the miracle I needed had happened. His reply was almost an anticlimax.

"Mr. Williamson, I have good news for you. We have a seat for you on the April 9 flight out of Montreal for Israel."

"Thank you, Mr. Telem, thank you!" I replied. "Yes, I'll be sure to let you know how the trip goes!" That was that. I was headed for Israel.

At 3:35 p.m., April 9, 1984, I boarded an Air Canada jet for the first leg of my journey to Israel. We arrived in Montreal at 4:45 p.m. All was well. I had a bit of time on my hands as my flight to Israel was not leaving until near midnight. Everything was well, that is, until I went to check in at the El Al ticket counter at 7:30 p.m. The crisis came after fifteen minutes of standing in line. I realized that I did not have my passport! Strangely enough, during the afternoon, while waiting in the airport, I had had a question go through my mind, "What would I do if I had to get something from Toronto before I left for Israel?" Had the Lord been preparing me? Did He really want me on this trip? Was I willing to return home without going to Israel? Had the Lord really said I would be in Jerusalem on the twelfth of April? For the next half hour I prayed over and over, "Not my will, Lord, but Thine be done."

At the El Al desk, I explained my problem and was directed to the Air Canada ticket counter. There I learned that flight 866 would be leaving Toronto for Montreal at 8:30 p.m. It was now just minutes before 8 p.m. I was then directed to the supervisor of the Air Canada baggage department. With heart pounding I quickly described my predicament.

"Can you help me?" I asked. Again I whispered to the Lord, "Not my will, but Thine be done!"

The supervisor calmly suggested that I contact my home in Toronto immediately and see if there was anyone who could take my passport to the airport. Without hesitation I called Marion. She was pleased to hear my voice, but distressed to hear about my passport problem. Sure enough, the passort was there at home. What should she do?

"Head immediately to the Air Canada counter for flight 866," I said. "We'll contact them to let them know you are on the way."

How thankful I was that our home was only

five minutes from the Toronto airport. With my call completed, the supervisor called Toronto and got hold of the baggage supervisor there. He was informed that Marion was on her way with the forgotten passport. I was now 8:03 p.m. At 8:13 p.m. Toronto called to let us know that the passport was now on flight 866.

"You'll have your passport soon," the Montreal supervisor assured me.

What a test that was! "Lord," I said, "You really do want me to go!"

The passport arrived at 9:15 p.m. When I called Marion, she gave a sigh of relief to know that everything was under control.

"Thank You, Heavenly Father!" I prayed. And then I added, "And thank you Air Canada for your help in this emergency!"

When the Lord had told me, "Now go" on the fifth of April, He also spoke to me from the remainder of that verse in Isaiah 30:8. It reads, "Write it on a tablet... that for the days to come it may be... a witness." I took it that I was to keep a record of the trip for some purpose. I often wonder about these kind of leadings only to be delighted later by the fruit my obedience produces. That record has provided the details for the account that follows.

Colonel Yehuda Levy and his wife, Nitza met me that evening at Ben Gurion Airport near Tel Aviv. We went directly to the Plaza Hotel where I was to stay. We spent an enjoyable half hour or so in one of the hotel restaurants. I had the pleasure of getting acquainted with Nitza and learning about the Levy's family. I also shared some details about my own family. One thing that stood out to me was the obvious joy of both

Nitza and Colonel Levy in talking about their two sons, Tzahal and Raanan, and their daughter, Odelia.

As we continued to converse, it became evident that the *Bridge of Love* program was felt very deeply by both Colonel Levy and his wife. In bidding one another good night, Nitza said she was looking forward to having me in their home later in the week. Colonel Levy added that he was making plans for me to join them for a special Passover celebration at his army base. I already felt very much at home.

During the hours of waking and sleeping because of jet lag that followed, many things were going through my mind. As a born-again, Spirit-filled Christian, I sensed that the Lord was asking me to give myself to Him in a different way than ever before. He was bringing me to a new understanding of His great and unconditional love for the world.

I was glad to have the next morning to rest in my hotel. During that quiet time with the Lord, I came across a passage in Isaiah 60:10, "Foreigners will rebuild your walls, and their kings will serve you." It took me back to a passage I had shared the previous week in staff devotions at church. I had spoken about the walls that Nehemiah was called to build. Here I was, a foreigner who had come to Israel with a deep longing to help her build her walls. I did not yet know exactly what God wanted me to do. I did know, however, that He would make it clear to me in the proper season.

That afternoon I enjoyed an informal business lunch with Colonel Levy and Naomi Band of the Plaza Hotel staff. The Plaza was to be one of the hotels where our tour guests would stay. Naomi related how she as a Jew had come to Israel four years previously from Great Britain. I shared with her how God had told me to pray for the peace of Jerusalem in a dream. She said she had met a couple from the Christian Embassy in Jerusalem with a similar story.

Later that afternoon, at Colonel Levy's office, I met Debbie and Carol from South Africa. We had quite a time exchanging stories of how we ended up in Israel. Colonel Levy described how he and I had met and his keen desire for me to come to Israel. As he spoke, the conviction that he was the contact person in Israel for whom I had been praying came close to the point of confirmation. I realized this man had a special call to bring people from many nations to the land of Israel. I commented that he would not just bring dozens or hundreds of people to Israel, but literally thousands. I added that people would bless him and that he would be a great blessing to them because God had chosen him and gifted him, not just with a business, but with a calling.

As I look back now, I see that this sense of calling has made the differnce in building this bridge of love together. I know he is called and he knows I am called. It was not our relationship that birthed our individual callings. Those were underway years before we met. What began when we met was a friendhsip through which our mutual callings could be fulfilled. Those days spent in Jerusalem were very important in that they confirmed for me the validity of each of our callings. By the time I arrived at Colonel Levy's office on the afternoon of April 15, I was able to say I had God's peace about forming a working relationship with him. With this matter settled, we began making plans for the first *Bridge of Love* convention. We felt that late January would be an excellent time for the convention as it would provide Canadians with the opportunity of taking a break from the sleet and snow in the lovely spring weather of Israel.

When I returned to Canada, I shared the details of the trip with my group of prayer partners. We decided to meet once a month to pray for Colonel Levy and his family and for Israel. We knew we must hear from the Lord regarding who should go to the first *Bridge of Love* convention the following January.

With the relationship with Colonel Levy and the *Bridge of Love* organization secured, I knew it was time to launch a Canadian counterpart organization. But where would the required money come from? I prayed a very simple prayer: "Lord Jesus, you know that Marion and I do not have the finances to incorporate Kerith. If you provide them supernaturally, then we will know we are to take this step." Not a week later I received a call from a friend who said that it was vital that we meet. The Lord had impressed this person to give us a certain amount of money. The gift was the exact amount we needed to register Kerith! The paper work was set in motion on August 1, 1984, and on August 14, 1984, *The Kerith Connection* was born.

It was exciting to watch as month by month one person then another would come to me and say that he or she had received confirmation from the Lord about joining the tour to Israel scheduled for January, 1985.

As with all good things, there were hours of testing. Colonel Levy called once, then twice, then a third time. Each time the news was worse than before. The plans we had laid out involving hundreds of visitors to Israel were not coming together. Large groups had booked in only to cancel. It finally came down to deciding whether or not to call off the convention. At this point I knew that our little group of nine were to be the entire convention. What boldness I felt. God was in this and I was going to obey His direction. I knew He would bless what He had called us to do. I told Colonel Levy that we were still coming even if no other groups showed up.

This is precisely what happened. Although ours was the only group, the tour was a marvellous success. It was on this tour that the Holy Spirit confirmed to my wife, Marion, her calling to this ministry to Israel. It was also at this time that the name for these tours to Israel was established. As we travelled around Israel, everyone kept commenting on all the almond trees we saw. We learned that the almond is the first tree to blossom in Israel each spring. This brought to my mind the story from Numbers, Chapter 17, about Aaron's rod that budded with almonds. As we thought of spring, we also thought of Easter and the Resurrection of Christ. This in turn reminded us of the resurrection of the land and people of Isreal. The word, "almond" kept coming up over and over again until one of our group, Dr. James Lunney, suggested that future trips be called, "Almond Tours."

Each day we met together for prayer. Each day we asked the Lord to show us how we could be a blessing to Israel. This He did at our closing banquet. It all happened when someone asked a question about planting trees in Israel. One thing led to another in rapid succession until

98

the "Bridge of Love Forest" was born. What excitement! We would go home and raise $10,000 through the *Kerith Connection*. It was our prayer that Christians everywhere would join us in this project. The forest would stand as a witness to our love for Israel. It would be our way of saying, "Israel, we care!" We were also participating in the fulfillment of God's word to Israel in Isaiah 41:19-20,

I will put in the desert the cedar and the acacia, the myrtle and the olive. I will set pines in the wasteland, the fir and the cypress together, so that people may see and know, may consider and understand, that the hand of the Lord has done this, that the Holy One of Isreal has created it.

Upon returning to Canada, I called together our prayer partners and began to share about the new project for planting trees in the "Bridge of Love Forest." The group could hardly contain their joy. I suggested a simple plan which challenged everyone present to have a 20/20 vision for the project. Each person would give $20.20 per month to the Jewish National Fund for the planting of trees in Israel. Then the miracle happened. In less than three minutes, the group members gave $2,000 in pledges towards the $10,000 project goal.

That night, as I looked back upon all the spiritual blessings I had received in the last few months, I understood Genesis 12:3 more than I ever have in my life, "I will bless those who bless you." I also had fresh insight into Paul's words from Romans 15:27, "For if the Gentiles have shared in the Jews' spiritual blessings, they owe it to the Jews to share with them their material blessings."

As I pen these words, I am reminded of Don

Krohn's words to me on July 13, 1981. Until now, they did not make much sense. He had said, "I see you, Clyde, in a desert with a stream coming out of your mouth. You are planting flowers in the desert and they are beginning to bloom." If we obey what God asks us to do, it is a "work of righteousness." This is because God initiates the work. I knew the "Bridge of Love Forest" was to be only the first of many such "works of righteousness" on behalf of Israel.

Colonel Levy had already initiated contact with the Jewish National Fund (JNF) in Toronto to let them know about the joint tree-planting project of the *Bridge of Love* and the *Kerith Connection*. He suggested I contact the JNF office and give them a report on how things were going. At that point, I knew very little about JNF. I did know, however, that I now had a strong desire to visit their office in Toronto. Upon arriving at 4600 Bathurst Street, I was greeted warmly and introduced to the Ontario Regional Emissary from Jerusalem for JNF, Colonel Yehoshua Bar-Am. I then met Yehuda Danzig who had just been appointed Executive Director for the Ontario Region. Next I met Monty Mazin, the new Associate Executive Director and Director of Public Relations.

Monty, a most enthusiastic individual, was bubbling over with questions about Kerith. Little did I know that he was recording the information I provided for a special certificate that would be awarded to *The Kerith Connection* at the 1985 JNF banquet held at the Royal York Hotel in Toronto.

That day I learned a great deal about the JNF. I discovered that the Jewish National Fund, the Keren Kayemeth Le'Israel, was founded at the

Fifth Zionist Congress in 1901 for the acquisition and development of land in Israel. Its activities came to include land purchases, reclamation, reforestation and road building.

Sixty years after its establishment, the JNF signed a covenant with the Government of Israel which made it the country's sole agent for land development.

The JNF is represented in forty countries, with its head office in Jerusalem. Planting trees is one of the more visible activities of the JNF in Israel today. Since the independence of Israel was declared in 1948, over 160 million trees have been planted. In a good year, the JNF plants some 5 million trees. In addition, to date more than 250,000 acres have been reclaimed from the swamps, deserts, and rocky hillsides of Israel. This all sounds to me like Isaiah 35:1, "The wilderness and the solitary place shall be glad for them; and the desert shall rejoice, and blossom as the rose" (KJV). What a thrill to be a part of the reclaiming of this land I love!

Within a few weeks Colonel Bar-Am called to invite me to sit as a guest on the National JNF Committee for the new "Plant-a-Tree" program. This program would enable every visitor from Canada to plant a tree in the Holy Land free of charge. What made it so exciting was that our 1986 Almond Tour was to be the first group to participate in the "Plant-a-Tree" program.

I cannot describe the joy our group felt in 1986 on Tu Bishvat (January 26) when we knelt on Israeli soil and with our own hands took tiny cypress saplings and planted them in the barren soil of the Baraket, the area near Tel Aviv where the "Bridge of Love Forest" is located. Tu Bishvat is the fifteenth day of the month of Shevat in the Jewish calendar. Israeli children and adults set this day aside at the beginning of each spring as a tree-planting holiday.

It was while I was on the "Plant-a-Tree" committee that I met Michael Goldstein, the National Vice President of JNF. After one of our early morning meetings, I asked Michael to tell me a little bit about his relationship with Colonel Levy. I did not anticipate his reply.

"You know, Clyde," he said, "Yehuda Levy is a very well-respected man in JNF. He has been one of our pioneers in seeing doors open into the Christian churches of Canada."

That statement went through my mind over and over. I rejoiced at how the Lord had led me to the man who had all the necessary experience and contacts both in my own nation and in the nation of Israel. Here in Canada he had been involved with the JNF with which I was now connected. There in Israel he had founded the *Bridge of Love* organization. How perfectly it all fit together.

Colonel Levy has now formed his own travel company specifically for the purpose of fulfilling his *Bridge of Love* vision internationally. When he called me to share this good news, he was quick to add, "You'll really like the name, Clyde. It is going to be called, *Lion of Juda Tours*." I was overjoyed with this splendid choice of a name. I began to pray that his new travel office in Tel Aviv would become a very special contact point for many thousands of travellers to Israel in the months and years ahead before Messiah comes.

If you wish to contact *Bridge of Love*, write,

Bridge of Love International
c/o Lion of Juda Tours,
27 Ben-Yehuda Street
Tel Aviv, Israel

If you wish to contact *The Kerith Connection*, write,

The Kerith Connection
Box 336,
Etobicoke, Ontario
Canada   M9C 4V3

God had established a practical link with Israel through which we could bless His people in a tangible way by doing "deeds of righteousness". All that remained was for the Esther Fast to be rebirthed. The Lord had yet to make clear the spiritual significance of the Esther Fast and its timing as a mandate for ongoing intercession until Messiah comes. These clarifications were not long in coming.

CHAPTER EIGHT

Strike Those Arrows Again!

In the fall of 1985 a group of ministers met together to pray for revival. The speaker, Pastor Craig Pitts, took his message from 2 Kings 13:17-19,

"Open the east window," he said, and he opened it. "Shoot!" Elisha said, and he shot. "The Lord's arrow of victory, the arrow of victory over Aram!" Elisha declared. "You will completely destroy the Arameans at Aphek."

Then he said, "Take the arrows," and the king took them. "Elisha told him, "Strike the ground." He struck it three times and stopped. The man of God was angry with him and said, "You should have struck the ground five or six times; then you would have defeated Aram and completely destroyed it. But now you will defeat it only three times."

His theme was, "Strike Those Arrows Again" – until the Lord comes. Craig had also written a chorus to these words. As we knelt in prayer that day, the Lord spoke to me. He said that His promises were like arrows and that we were to strike them again and again through prayer. He said that the Esther Fast was a bundle of arrows and that each year we observed it, we were striking the ground again and again, thus ensuring the final victory.

We had not held an Esther Fast in 1984 or 1985. It was observed locally in 1986 in obedience to this call to strike the arrows again. We held it during the Feast of Purim according to the Jewish Calendar. This is the time Queen Esther's victory is celebrated each year. This timing somehow did not seem right, and so I continued to pray for further clarification. The answer came only after much prayer and many months of waiting.

On the morning of August 17, 1986, while reading Mrs. Charles Cowman's *Streams in the Desert*, I came across these words from Acts 27:25, "I believe God, that it shall be even as it was told me" (KJV). The more I meditated on this verse, the more I knew it was a key to the timing of the Esther Fast. "It shall be" was speaking of the future. "Even as it was told me" was speaking of the past. I got out a copy of the 1983 Esther Fast scroll and a 1983 calendar to check the days on which we had celebrated the Esther Fast. Then I found a calendar for the coming year, 1987. What I discovered paralleled my experience in 1983 perfectly. In 1983, the fast was celebrated on the first, second, and third of April which fell on the fourth, fifth, and sixth days of Passover. In 1983, these dates also represented Good Friday, Holy Saturday, and Easter Sunday. As I compared 1983 to 1987, my eyes nearly popped out of my head. I looked for the fourth, fifth, and sixth days of Passover in 1987. Once again they fell on Good Friday, Holy Saturday, and Easter Sunday! "It shall be even as it was told me." It was at this point I knew the Esther Fast should be celebrated each year until Messiah comes, on the fourth, fifth, and sixth days of Passover on the Jewish Calendar, whether these days fall on Easter weekend or not.

"Strike Those Arrows Again" was only a chorus in Craig Pitts' mind that day he ministered from 2 Kings, chapter 13. In sharing with him about what had happened to me in prayer that morning, I asked if he would give permission to use this chorus on the back of the 1986 Esther Fast scroll. He said he sensed there was more than just a chorus there and asked me to pray and see what the Lord would give him.

The next day Craig called with great excitement to say that the Lord had given him an entire song. I asked if he would sing it over the telephone. As he did, tears of joy filled my eyes. The music and words to this song have been included at the back of this book.

In 1984, the Lord gave us twenty-eight prayer partners to join in this vision for end-time intercession. In 1985, He added several hundred more intercessors to the company. Then, in 1986, He placed in my heart the desire to write this book and sow its message all over the world. At the same time, the Lord prompted me to go on a twenty-one-day Daniel fast.

In all my years of Christian ministry, no passage has fascinated me more than Daniel, chapter 9. I have often preached a message entitled, "The Word, the Prayer, and the Vision" from this chapter. In the context of my life, Daniel 9:1-3 has become more and more significant:

> In the first year of Darius son of Xerxes (a Mede by descent), who was made ruler over the Babylonian kingdom – in the first year of his reign, I, Daniel, understood from the Scriptures, according to the word of the Lord given to Jeremiah the

prophet, that the desolation of Jerusalem would last seventy years. So I turned to the Lord God and pleaded with Him in prayer and petition, in fasting, and in sackcloth and ashes.

We see here, that one day, Daniel was reading the prophecy of Jeremiah. He read Jeremiah's words that the Jews would be held in Babylon in captivity for seventy years and then released. We can read this same prediction in Jeremiah 25:11, "The whole country will become a desolate wasteland, and these nations will serve the king of Babylon seventy years" (see also Jeremiah 29:10). As Daniel looked at his calendar, he realized the hour was almost at hand for this word to be fulfilled. Daniel's response was not just a response of the intellect, it was a yielding of his heart to the call of the Spirit of God to pray on behalf of himself and his people.

This is the Daniel that was faithful in prayer three times a day. This is the one who was delivered from the lion's den. This is the man who knew not only how to talk to God, but also how to hear from God in dreams, visions, and through the Holy Scriptures. This great man of God got down on his knees to confess his sins in sackcloth and ashes. He laboured in prayer to make sure he was forgiven, to make sure his heart was pure before God. Following the confession of his own sins, Daniel got down before the Lord and began to weep and mourn over the sins of his nation and ask God to forgive them.

I have experienced this passage over and over again. I see modern Israel and the modern church in desperate need of people like Daniel to stand in the gap. I hear God's call for intercessors recorded in Ezekiel 22:30,

> I looked for a man among them who would build up the wall and stand before me in the gap on behalf of the land so I would not have to destroy it, but I found none.

This call for prayer warriors, for men and women and young people who are willing to "stand in the gap" as intercessors still goes forth today. God is searching for people who will call upon Him for mercy, first for their own sins, and then for the sins of their nation. It is only through intercessors such as these that God can turn back the tide of iniquity which has flooded the earth.

God is seeking for Daniels. He is searching for a humble people who are willing to confess their sins and seek His forgiveness. He longs to see those whose hearts are made right, pore over the promises of God that are as yet unfulfilled as Daniel did over the words of Jeremiah. God by His Spirit reveals these promises one at a time as we yield ourselves to the study of His Word. We, too, will become like Daniel and as we read His word, passages that He is calling us to pray over will stand out to us. We will experience a partnership with the Lord as Daniel did in praying through these promises. This is the chemistry of prayer. It is the chemistry of end-time intercession.

This is not to say that we are in any way going to bring about the fulfillment of these things. They will come about in God's perfect time. And yet, in the Scriptures, we read Israel was called to "ask... of the Lord rain *in the time of the latter rain*" (Zechariah 10:1, KJV, emphasis mine). Through prayer, God allows His children to play a vital part in the fulfillment of His purposes.

Like Daniel of old we have opened the ancient scrolls. We have seen the unfulfilled words of the prophets concerning Israel. We see the hour is at hand for many of these words to be fulfilled, words such as Isaiah 2:2-4,

> In the last days the mountain of the Lord's temple will be established as chief among the mountains; it will be raised above the hills, and all nations will stream to it.
> Many peoples will come and say, "Come let us go up to the mountain of the Lord, to the house of the God of Jacob. He will teach us his ways, so that we may walk in his paths." The law will go out from Zion, the word of the Lord from Jerusalem.
> He will come and judge between the nations and settle disputes for many peoples. They will beat their swords into plowshares and their spears into pruning hooks. Nation will not take up sword against nation, nor will they train for war anymore.

Church of Jesus Christ, the hour has come for end-time fasting and prayer. It is time for believers everywhere throughout the globe to request from God the return of his ancient people to their homeland. Our mandate is fourfold:

1. Pray for the release of the Jewish people from bondage.

2. Pray for the lifting up of the name of the Lord in the midst of Israel.

3. Pray for Israel to be set free in spirit to fulfill her mission which has been commanded in Holy Scripture (Isaiah 52:5-10).

4. Pray that the Church of Jesus Christ be brought into her fullest liberty to be a mighty voice in all the earth.

This call is for an Esther Fast, an absolute fast of three days: "Do not eat or drink for three days, night or day" (Esther 4:16). Further instructions on fasting are provided in the Appendices. The timing of the fast is to be from sundown on the third day of Passover to sundown on the sixth day of Passover, annually, until Messiah comes. The Appendices provide the annual dates for the Esther Fast until the year 2000.

There are three aspects to the spiritual significance of the Esther Fast. First it is a fast like Queen Esther undertook to deliver her people from total destruction at the hand of the wicked Haman. We are praying for the protection of the nation of Israel from the myriad of forces in today's world that would rejoice to see her annihilated.

Second it is to be held during Passover, the time when God's people recall their deliverance from bondage in Egypt. We are praying for a new exodus of the Jews out of the "land of the north" (the Soviet Union) and "all the countries where he has banished them" (Jeremiah 23:8).

Third, the fast will begin each year at sundown on the third day of Passover, the day that Jesus rose from the dead. We pray for the resurrection of God's people, Israel in accordance with the promise of Isaiah 66:8,10,

Who has ever heard of such a thing? Can a country be born in a day or a nation be brought forth in a moment? Yet no sooner is Zion in labour than she gives birth to her children....

Rejoice with Jerusalem and be glad for her, all you who love her; rejoice greatly with her, all you who mourn over her.

Who may participate in the Esther Fast? It is for all God's people who sense the liberty and the calling to be part of this worldwide season of intercession. This fast began as a call to fervent prayer placed upon the hearts of Canadians. It

110

is now a challenge to every believer around the world to break forth in strong intercession for the greatest move of God's Holy Spirit ever known to mankind. It will be on these days of fasting and prayer that we will pore over the Holy Scriptures like Daniel did. It will be on these days of baring our hearts before God that we will begin to confess our sins and the sins of our nations.

Believers everywhere are catching the ongoing vision of the Esther Fast Mandate. They are determined to pray through the promises of God for the Release, Return, Restoration, and Revival of Israel and the Church until Messiah comes!

The mandate is before us.

The timing is clear.

Let us unite our hearts in intercession each year at Passover and, "Strike Those Arrows Again" until the victory comes!

Map courtesy of the Israeli Government Tourist Office.

Organizations
Assisting Soviet Jews

CANADA

Canadian Committee
for Soviet Jewry,
1590 Avenue Docteur Penfield
MONTREAL, P.Q.,
Canada H3G 1C5

Committee for Soviet Jewry,
Canadian Jewish Congress,
4600 Bathurst Street,
WILLOWDALE, Ontario,
Canada M2R 3V2

ISRAEL

Centre for Information
on Soviet Jewry
Alkali 9,
JERUSALEM, Israel

The International Christian
Embassy, Jerusalem
P.O. Box 1192
JERUSALEM, Israel

Christian Action For Israel,
Mr. Claude Duvernoy,
International Founder,
111 Uziel Street,
JERUSALEM, Israel

Jerusalem Vistas and
International Vistas,
Jay and Meridel Rawlings,
Directors and Founders,
Box 8232
JERUSALEM, 91081, Israel

NETHERLANDS

Christian Help for
Prisoners of Conscience,
"Let My People Go",
Postbus 80,
1619 ZH Andijk,
Netherlands

UNITED STATES

Union of Councils
for Soviet Jews,
1819 H. Street, N.W.,
WASHINGTON, D.C.,
U.S.A. 20006

National Conference
on Soviet Jewry,
10 East 40th Street,
NEW YORK, N.Y.,
U.S.A. 16016

GREAT BRITAIN

Keston College
Heathfield Road
KESTON, Kent,
U.K. BR2 6B4

National Council for Soviet
Jewry of U.K. and Ireland,
183-189 Finchley Road
LONDON, U.K. NW3 6LD

SOUTH AFRICA

Christian Action for Israel,
Mr. Basil Jacobs,
P.O. Box 11392,
Vlaeberg,
CAPETOWN, 8010
Republic of South Africa

FRANCE

Congress Juif Mondiale,
78, Avenue des Champs-Elysee's,
PARIS 75008, France

WEST GERMANY

U.S.S.R. News Brief,
Das Land und die Welt e.V.,
Sendlivgerstrasse 37,
800 Munchen 2, B.R.D.

Jewish National Fund
Offices

CANADA

National Office,
Jewish National Fund
1980 Sherbrooke Street West,
Suite 330,
MONTREAL, Quebec H3H 2M7
Tel. (514) 934-0313

Jewish National Fund
4600 Bathurst Street,
Suite 238,
WILLOWDALE, Ontario
M2R 3V3
Tel. (416) 638-7200

Jewish National Fund
905 West 41st Avenue,
VANCOUVER, B.C. V5Z 2N7
Tel. (604) 266-4191

ARGENTINA

Fondo de Intercâmbio Agrario
Argention-Israeli (F.I.A.A.I.)
Corrientes 2294 5 piso
BUENOS AIRES 1046
Argentina
Tel. 485683 & 483695

SOUTH AFRICA

Jewish National Fund,
P.O.B. 18,
JOHANNESBURG 2000
Republic of South Africa
Tel. (011) 337-3000

UNITED STATES

National Office,
Jewish National Fund, Inc.
42 East 69th Street,
NEW YORK, N.Y. 10021
Tel. (212) 879-9300

Jewish National Fund
6380 Wilshire Blvd.,
Suite 1108,
LOS ANGELES, Cal. 90048
Tel. (213) 655-8100

ISRAEL

National Institutions
Buildings
Keren Kayemeth Street
P.O.B. 283
91002 JERUSALEM, Israel
Tel. (02) 240251

AUSTRALIA

Jewish National Fund,
79-85 Oxford Street
Bondi Junction
SYDNEY,
N.S.W. 2022
Tel. 389-5466

NEW ZEALAND

Jewish National Fund,
P.O.B. 3217
WELLINGTON, New Zealand

Dates for the Esther Fast, 1987-2000

Year	First Day of Passover	Esther Fast Starts Sundown This Day	Esther Fast Days
1987	April 14	April 16	April 17-19
1988	April 2	April 4	April 5-7
1989	April 20	April 22	April 23-25
1990	April 10	April 12	April 13-15
1991	March 30	April 1	April 2-4
1992	April 18	April 20	April 21-23
1993	April 6	April 8	April 9-11
1994	March 27	March 29	Mar. 30 - Apr. 1
1995	April 15	April 17	April 18-20
1996	April 4	April 6	April 7-9
1997	April 22	April 24	April 25-27
1998	April 11	April 13	April 14-16
1999	April 1	April 3	April 4-6
2000	April 20	April 22	April 23-25

Instructions

for Prayer and Fasting

1. During the days of the fast, from sundown on the third day of Passover to sundown on the sixth day, eat or drink absolutely nothing. The only exception is the taking of Holy Communion.

2. If you are not used to fasting, why not try one or two, one-day fasts in the month before you attempt the Esther Fast.

3. You should not fast if you are pregnant, or suffering from illness or some other medical condition.

4. When you complete your fast, come off it gradually. Do not eat meat for the first day and a half after your fast. When you begin to eat, have light foods like juices, soup, bread, crackers, and so forth. Gradually add more protein foods until you are eating normally again at the end of the second day.

5. Be sure to spend extra time in prayer and in the Scriptures. This is the purpose of fasting so that you can devote yourself without reservation to seeking God in prayer. Study the verses given at the end of chapter 5 dealing with Israel's return to the land.

6. Be specific in your prayers. See the "Prayer for Oppressed Jews" found in chapter 5 and the list of items for prayer given in the Esther

Fast Mandate in chapter 8. As well, you could contact your Christian friends who are doing the fast and exchange prayer requests with them. The following is a brief outline of some categories in which to pray.

a. Pray for forgiveness for yourself and also for the sins of your nation as Daniel did (chapter 9).

b. Pray for God's direction in your life and ministry.

c. Pray for reconciliation in your own personal relationships as well as between groups, regions, and nations.

d. Pray specifically about your own ministry in the body of Christ. Ask God to direct and empower you so that you may be a blessing using the gifts He has given you in ministry to others.

e. Pray so as to deepen your commitment as you yield yourself to the Lord in every area of your life.

"Strike Those Arrows Again!"

From: II Kings 13: 17-19 & Isaiah 52: 7-10   Words & Music By Craig F. Pitts

(Copyright 1985 by Craig F. Pitts)

Bibliography

The Death and Resurrection of Israel
  by Arthur W. Kac
  (Baltimore: King Brothers, Inc., 1969).
Exodus II, Let My People Go!
  by Steve Lightle with Eberhard Muhlan
  and Katie Fortune
  (Kingwood, Texas: Hunter Books, 1983).
Fishers and Hunters
  by Jay and Meridel Rawlings
  (Jerusalem: International Vistas, 1985).
Gates of Brass
  by Jay and Meridel Rawlings
  (Jerusalem: International Vistas, 1985).
A Gentile with the Heart of a Jew:
  G. Douglas Young, A Biography
  by Calvin B. Hanson
  (Nyack, New York: Parson Publishing, 1979).
God's Chosen Fast
  by Arthur Wallis (Elgin, Ontario:
  Christian Literature Crusade, 1979).
None Is Too Many, Canada and the
  Jews of Europe, 1933-1948
  by Irving Abella and Harold Troper (Toronto:
  Lester and Orpen Dennys Ltd., 1983).
Shcharansky: Hero of Our Time
  by Martin Gilbert
  (New York: Viking, 1986).
What Christians Should Know About
  Jews and Judaism
  by Rabbi Yechiel Eckstein
  (Waco, Texas: Word Books, 1984).